A Ten Year War

by Jacob A. Riis

CONTENTS

CHAP.

A TEN YEARS' WAR

I

THE BATTLE WITH THE SLUM

The slum is as old as civilization. Civilization implies a race, to get ahead. In a race there are usually some who for one cause or another cannot keep up, or are thrust out from among their fellows. They fall behind, and when they have been left far in the rear they lose hope and ambition, and give up. Thenceforward, if left to their own resources, they are the victims, not the masters, of their environment; and it is a bad master. They drag one another always farther down. The bad environment becomes the heredity of the next generation. Then, given the crowd, you have the slum ready-made.

The battle with the slum began the day civilization recognized in it her enemy. It was a losing fight until conscience joined forces with fear and self-interest against it. When common sense and the golden rule obtain among men as a rule of practice, it will be over. The two have not always been classed together, but here they are plainly seen to belong together. Justice to the individual is accepted in theory as the only safe groundwork of the commonwealth. When it is practiced in dealing with the slum, there will shortly be no slum. We need not wait for the millennium, to get rid of it. We can do it now. All that is required is that it shall not be left to itself. That is justice to it and to us, since its grievous ailment is that it cannot help itself. When a man is drowning, the thing to do is to pull him out of the water; afterward there will be time for talking it over. We got at it the other way in dealing with our social problems. The doctrinaires had their day, and they decided to let bad enough alone; that it was unsafe to interfere with "causes that operate sociologically," as one survivor of these unfittest put it to me. It was a piece of scientific humbug that cost the age which listened to it dear. "Causes that operate sociologically" are the opportunity of the political and every other kind of scamp who trades upon the depravity and helplessness of the slum, and the refuge of the pessimist who is useless in the fight against them. We have not done yet paying the bills he ran up for us. Some time since we turned to, to pull the drowning man out, and it was time. A little while longer, and we should have been in danger of being dragged down with him.

The slum complaint had been chronic in all ages, but the great changes which the nineteenth century saw, the new industry, political freedom, brought on an acute attack which threatened to become fatal. Too many of us had supposed that, built as our commonwealth was on universal suffrage, it would be proof against the complaints that harassed older states; but in fact it turned out that there was extra hazard in that. Having solemnly resolved that all men are created equal and have certain inalienable rights, among them life, liberty, and the pursuit of happiness, we shut our eyes and waited for the formula to work. It was as if a man with a cold should take the doctor's prescription to bed with him, expecting it to cure him. The formula was all right, but merely repeating it worked no cure. When, after a hundred years, we opened our eyes, it was upon sixty cents a day as the living wage of the working-woman in our cities; upon "knee pants" at forty cents a dozen for the making; upon the Potter's Field taking tithe of our city life, ten per cent, each year for the trench, truly the Lost Tenth of the slum. Our country had grown great and rich; through our ports was poured food for the millions of Europe. But in the back streets multitudes huddled in ignorance and want. The foreign oppressor had been vanquished, the fetters stricken from the black man at home; but his white brother, in his bitter plight, sent up a cry of distress that had in it a distinct note of menace. Political freedom we had won; but the problem of helpless poverty, grown vast with the added offscourings of the Old World, mocked us, unsolved. Liberty at sixty cents a day set presently its stamp upon the government of our cities, and it became the scandal and the peril of our political system.

So the battle began. Three times since the war that absorbed the nation's energies and attention had the slum confronted us in New York with its challenge. In the darkest days of the great struggle it was the treacherous mob; later on, the threat of the cholera, which found swine foraging in the streets as the only scavengers, and a swarming host, but little above the hog in its appetites and in the quality of the shelter afforded it, peopling the back alleys. Still later, the mob, caught looting the city's treasury with its idol, the thief Tweed, at its head, drunk with power and plunder, had insolently defied the outraged community to do its worst. There were meetings and protests. The rascals were turned out for a season; the arch-thief died in jail. I see him now, going through the gloomy portals of the Tombs, whither, as a newspaper reporter, I had gone with him, his stubborn head held high as ever.

I asked myself more than once, at the time when the vile prison was torn down, whether the comic clamor to have the ugly old gates preserved and set up in Central Park had anything to do with the memory of the "martyred" thief, or whether it was in joyful celebration of the fact that others had escaped. His name is even now one to conjure with in the Sixth Ward. He never "squealed," and he was "so good to the poor"--evidence that the slum is not laid by the heels by merely destroying Five Points and the Mulberry Bend. There are other fights to be fought in that war, other victories to be won, and it is slow work. It was nearly ten years after the great robbery before decency got the upper grip in good earnest. That was when the civic conscience awoke in 1879.

In that year the slum was arraigned in the churches. The sad and shameful story was told of how it grew and was fostered by avarice, that saw in the homeless crowds from over the sea only a chance for business, and exploited them to the uttermost, making sometimes a hundred per cent, on the capital invested,--always most out of the worst houses, from the tenants of which "nothing was expected" save that they pay the usurious rents; how Christianity, citizenship, human fellowship, shook their skirts clear of the rabble that was only good enough to fill the greedy purse, and how the rabble, left to itself, improved such opportunities as it found after such fashion as it knew; how it ran elections merely to count its thugs in, and fattened at the public crib; and how the whole evil thing had its root in the tenements, where the home had ceased to be sacred,--those dark and deadly dens in which the family ideal was tortured to death, and character was smothered; in which children were "damned rather than born" into the world, thus realizing a slum kind of foreordination to torment, happily brief in many cases. The Tenement House Committee long afterward called the worst of the barracks "infant slaughter houses," and showed, by reference to the mortality lists, that they killed one in every five babies born in them.

The story shocked the town into action. Plans for a better kind of tenement were called for, and a premium was put on every ray of light and breath of air that could be let into it. Money was raised to build model houses, and a bill to give the health authorities summary powers in dealing with tenements was sent to the legislature. The landlords held it up until the last day of the session, when it was forced through by an angered public opinion. The power of the cabal was broken. The landlords had found their Waterloo. Many of them got rid of their property, which in a large number of cases they had never seen, and tried to forget the source of their ill-gotten wealth. Light and air did find their way into the tenements in a half-hearted fashion, and we began to count the tenants as "souls." That is one of our milestones in the history of New York. They were never reckoned so before; no one ever thought of them as "souls." So, restored to human fellowship, in the twilight of the air shaft that had penetrated to their dens, the first Tenement House Committee was able to make them out "better than the houses" they lived in, and a long step forward was taken. The Mulberry Bend, the wicked core of the "bloody Sixth Ward," was marked for destruction, and all slumdom held its breath to see it go. With that gone, it seemed as if the old days must be gone too, never to return. There would not be another Mulberry Bend. As long as it stood, there was yet a chance. The slum had backing, as it were.

The civic conscience was not very robust yet, and required many and protracted naps. It slumbered fitfully eight long years, waking up now and then with a start, while the politicians did their best to lull it back to its slumbers. I wondered often, in those years of delay, if it was just plain stupidity that kept the politicians from spending the money which the law had put within their grasp; for with every year that passed a million dollars that could have been used for small park purposes was lost. But they were wiser than I. I understood when I saw the changes which letting in the sunshine worked. We had all believed it, but they knew it all along. At the same time, they lost none of the chances that offered. They helped the landlords, who considered themselves greatly aggrieved because their property was thereafter to front on a park instead of a pigsty, to transfer the whole assessment of half a million dollars for park benefit to the city. They undid in less than six weeks what it had taken considerably more than six years to do; but the park was cheap at the price. We could afford to pay all it cost to wake us up. When finally, upon the wave of wrath excited by the Parkhurst and Lexow disclosures, reform came with a shock that dislodged Tammany, it found us wide awake, and, it must be admitted, not a little astonished at our sudden access of righteousness.

The battle went against the slum in the three years that followed, until it found backing in the "odium of reform" that became the issue in the municipal organization of the greater city. Tammany made notes. Of what was done, how it was done, and why, during those years, I shall have occasion to speak further in these pages. Here I wish to measure the stretch we have come since I wrote "How the Other Half Lives," ten years ago. Some of it we came plodding, and some at full speed; some of it in the face of every obstacle that could be thrown in our way, wresting victory from defeat at every step; some of it with the enemy on the run. Take it altogether, it is a long way. Most of it will not have to be traveled over again. The engine of municipal progress, once started as it has been in New York, may slip many a cog with Tammany as the engineer; it may even be stopped for a season; but it can never be made to work backward. Even Tammany knows that, and is building the schools she so long neglected, and so is hastening the day when she shall be but an unsavory memory.

How we strove for those schools, to no purpose! Our arguments, our anger, the anxious pleading of philanthropists who saw the young on the East Side going to ruin, the warning year after year of the superintendent of schools that the compulsory education law was but an empty mockery where it was most needed, the knocking of uncounted thousands of children for whom there was no room,--uncounted in sober fact; there was not even a way of finding out how many were adrift,--brought only the response that the tax rate must be kept down. Kept down it was. "Waste" was successfully averted at the spigot; at the bunghole it went on unchecked. In a swarming population like that you must have either schools or jails, and the jails waxed fat with the overflow. The East Side, that had been orderly, became a hotbed of child crime. And when, in answer to the charge made by a legislative committee that the father forced his child into the shop, on a perjured age certificate, to labor when he ought to have been at play, that father, bent and heavy-eyed with unceasing toil, flung back the charge with the bitter reproach that we gave him no other choice, that it was either the street or the shop for his boy, and that perjury for him was cheaper than the ruin of the child, we were mute. What, indeed, was there to say? The crime was ours, not his. That was but yesterday. To-day we can count the months to the time when every child who knocks shall find a seat in our schools. We have a school census to tell us of the need. In that most crowded neighborhood in all the world, where the superintendent lately pleaded in vain for three new schools, five have been built, the finest in this or any other land,--great, light, and airy structures, with playgrounds on the roof; and all over the city the like are going up. The briefest of our laws, every word of which is like the blow of a hammer driving the nails home in the coffin of the bad old days, says that never one shall be built without its playground. So the boy is coming to his rights.

The streets are cleaned,--not necessarily clean just now; Colonel Waring is dead, with his doctrine of putting a man instead of a voter behind every broom, killed by politics, he and his doctrine both,--but cleaned. The slum has even been washed. We tried that on Hester Street years ago, in the age of cobblestone pavements, and the result fairly frightened us. I remember the indignant reply of a well-known citizen, a man of large business responsibility and experience in the handling of men, to whom the office of street-cleaning commissioner had been offered, when I asked him if he would accept. "I have lived," he said, "a blameless life for forty years, and have a character in the community. I cannot afford--no man with a reputation can afford--to hold that office; it will surely wreck it." That was then. It made Colonel Waring's reputation. He took the trucks from the streets. Tammany, in a brief interregnum of vigor under Mayor Grant, had laid the axe to the unsightly telegraph poles and begun to pave the streets with asphalt, but it left the trucks and the ash barrels to Colonel Waring as hopeless. Trucks have votes; at least their drivers have. Now that they are gone, the drivers would be the last to bring them back; for they have children, too, and the rescued streets gave them their first playground. Perilous, begrudged by policeman and storekeeper, though it was, it was still a playground.

But one is coming in which the boy shall rule unchallenged. The Mulberry Bend Park kept its promise. Before the sod was laid in it two more were under way in the thickest of the tenement house crowding, and each, under the law which brought them into existence, is to be laid out in part as a playground. They are not yet finished, but they will be; for the people have taken to the idea, and the politician has made a note of the fact. He saw a great light when the play piers were opened. In half a dozen localities where the slum was striking its roots deep into the soil such piers are now being built, and land is being acquired for small parks. We shall yet settle the "causes that operated sociologically" on the boy with a lawn mower and a sand heap. You have got your boy, and the heredity of the next one, when you can order his setting.

Even while I am writing, a bill is urged in the legislature to build in every senatorial district in the city a gymnasium and a public bath. It matters little whether it passes at this session or not. The important thing is that it is there. The rest will follow. A people's club is being organized, to crowd out the saloon that has had a monopoly of the brightness and the cheer in the tenement streets too long. The labor unions are bestirring themselves to deal with the sweating curse, and the gospel of less law and more enforcement sits enthroned at Albany. Theodore Roosevelt will teach us again Jefferson's forgotten lesson, that "the whole art of government consists in being honest." With a back door to every ordinance that touched the lives of the people, if indeed the whole thing was not the subject of open ridicule or the vehicle of official blackmail, it seemed as if we had provided a perfect municipal machinery for bringing the law into contempt with the young, and so for wrecking citizenship by the shortest cut.

Of free soup there is an end. It was never food for free men. The last spoonful was ladled out by yellow journalism with the certificate of the men who fought Roosevelt and reform in the police board that it was good. It is not likely that it will ever plague us again. Our experience has taught us a new reading of the old word that charity covers a multitude of sins. It does. Uncovering some of them has kept us busy since our conscience awoke, and there are more left. The worst of them all, that awful parody on municipal charity, the police station lodging room, is gone, after twenty years of persistent attack upon the foul dens,--years during which they were arraigned, condemned, indicted by every authority having jurisdiction, all to no purpose. The stale beer dives went with them and with the Bend, and the grip of the tramp on our throat has been loosened. We shall not easily throw it off altogether, for the tramp has a vote, too, for which Tammany, with admirable ingenuity, has found a new use, since the ante-election inspection of lodging houses has made them less available for colonization purposes than they were. Perhaps I should say a new way of very old use. It is simplicity itself. Instead of keeping tramps in hired lodgings for weeks at a daily outlay, the new way is to send them all to the island on short commitments during the canvass, and vote them from there en bloc at the city's expense. Time and education must solve that, like so many other problems which the slum has thrust upon us. They are the forces upon which, when we have gone as far as our present supply of steam will carry us, we must always fall back; and this we may do with confidence so long as we keep stirring, if it is only marking time, as now. It is in the retrospect that one sees how far we have come, after all, and from that gathers courage for the rest of the way. Twenty-nine years have passed since I slept in a police station lodging house, a lonely lad, and was robbed, beaten, and thrown out for protesting; and when the vagrant cur that had joined its homelessness to mine, and had sat all night at the door waiting for me to come out,--it had been clubbed away the night before,--snarled and showed its teeth at the doorman, raging and impotent I saw it beaten to death on the step. I little dreamed then that the friendless beast, dead, should prove the undoing of the monstrous wrong done by the maintenance of these evil holes to every helpless man and woman who was without shelter in New York; but it did. It was after an inspection of the lodging rooms, when I stood with Theodore Roosevelt, then president of the police board, in the one where I had slept that night, and told him of it, that he swore they should go. And go they did, as did so many another abuse in those two years of honest purpose and effort. I hated them. It may not have been a very high motive to furnish power for municipal reform; but we had tried every other way, and none of them worked. Arbitration is good, but there are times when it becomes necessary to knock a man down and arbitrate sitting on him, and this was such a time. It was what we started out to do with the rear tenements, the worst of the slum barracks, and it would have been better had we kept on that track. I have always maintained that we made a false move when we stopped to discuss damages with the landlord, or to hear his side of it at all. His share in it was our grievance; it blocked the mortality records with its burden of human woe. The damage was all ours, the profit all his. If there are damages to collect, he should foot the bill, not we. Vested rights are to be protected, but no man has a right to be protected in killing his neighbor.

However, they are down, the worst of them. The community has asserted its right to destroy tenements that destroy life, and for that cause. We bought the slum off in the Mulberry Bend at its own figure. On the rear tenements we set the price, and set it low. It was a long step. Bottle Alley is gone, and Bandits' Roost. Bone Alley, Thieves' Alley, and Kerosene Row,--they are all gone. Hell's Kitchen and Poverty Gap have acquired standards of decency; Poverty Gap has risen even to the height of neckties. The time is fresh in my recollection when a different kind of necktie was its pride; when the boy murderer--he was barely nineteen--who wore it on the gallows took leave of the captain of detectives with the cheerful invitation to "come over to the wake. They will have a high old time." And the event fully redeemed the promise. The whole Gap turned out to do the dead bully honor. I have not heard from the Gap, and hardly from Hell's Kitchen, in five years. The last news from the Kitchen was when the thin wedge of a column of negroes, in their uptown migration, tried to squeeze in, and provoked a race war; but that in fairness should not be laid up against it. In certain local aspects it might be accounted a sacred duty; as much so as to get drunk and provoke a fight on the anniversary of the battle of the Boyne. But on the whole the Kitchen has grown orderly. The gang rarely beats a policeman nowadays, and it has not killed one in a long while.

So, one after another, the outworks of the slum have been taken. It has been beaten in many battles; but its reserves are unimpaired. More tenements are being built every day on twenty-five-foot lots, and however watchfully such a house is planned, if it is to return to the builder the profit he seeks, it will have that within it which, the moment the grasp of official sanitary supervision is loosened, must summon up the ghost of the slum. The common type of tenement to-day is the double-decker, and the double-decker is hopeless. In it the crowding goes on at a constantly increasing rate. This is the sore spot, and as against it all the rest seems often enough unavailing. Yet it cannot be. It is true that the home, about which all that is to work for permanent progress must cluster, is struggling against desperate odds in the tenement, and that the struggle has been reflected in the morals of the people, in the corruption of the young, to an alarming extent; but it must be that the higher standards now set up on every hand, in the cleaner streets, in the better schools, in the parks and the clubs, in the settlements, and in the thousand and one agencies for good that touch and help the lives of the poor at as many points, will tell at no distant day, and react upon the homes and upon their builders. To any one who knew the East Side, for instance, ten years ago, the difference between that day and this in the appearance of the children whom he sees there must be striking. Rags and dirt are now the exception rather than the rule. Perhaps the statement is a trifle too strong as to the dirt; but dirt is not harmful except when coupled with rags; it can be washed off, and nowadays is washed off where such a thing would have been considered affectation in the days that were. Soap and water have worked a visible cure already, that must go more than skin-deep. They are moral agents of the first value in the slum. And the day must come when rapid transit will cease to be a football between contending forces in a city of three million people, and the reason for the outrageous crowding will cease to exist with the scattering of the centres of production to the suburb. That day may be a long way off, measured by the impatience of the philanthropist, but it is bound to come. Meanwhile, philanthropy is not sitting idle and waiting. It is building tenements on the humane plan that wipes out the lines of the twenty-five-foot lot, and lets in sunshine and air and hope. It is putting up hotels deserving of the name for the army that but just now had no other home than the cheap lodging houses which Inspector Byrnes fitly called "nurseries of crime." These also are standards from which there is no backing down, even if coming up to them is slow work: and they are here to stay, for they pay. That is the test. Not charity, but justice,--that is the gospel which they preach.

Flushed with the success of many victories, we challenged the slum to a fight to the finish a year ago, and bade it come on. It came on. On our side fought the bravest and best. The man who marshaled the citizen forces for their candidate had been foremost in building homes, in erecting baths for the people, in directing the self-sacrificing labors of the oldest and worthiest of the agencies for improving the condition of the poor. With him battled men who had given lives of patient study and effort to the cause of helping their fellow men. Shoulder to shoulder with them stood the thoughtful workingman from the East Side tenement. The slum, too, marshaled its forces. Tammany produced her notes. She pointed to the increased tax rate, showed what it had cost to build schools and parks and to clean house, and called it criminal recklessness. The issue was made sharp and clear. The war cry of the slum was characteristic: "To hell with reform!" We all remember the result. Politics interfered, and turned victory into defeat. We were beaten. I shall never forget that election night. I walked home through the Bowery in the midnight hour, and saw it gorging itself, like a starved wolf, upon the promise of the morrow. Drunken men and women sat in every doorway, howling ribald songs and curses. Hard faces I had not seen for years showed themselves about the dives. The mob made merry after its fashion. The old days were coming back. Reform was dead, and decency with it.

A year later, I passed that same way on the night of election. The scene was strangely changed. The street was unusually quiet for such a time. Men stood in groups about the saloons, and talked in whispers, with serious faces. The name of Roosevelt was heard on every hand. The dives were running, but there was no shouting, and violence was discouraged. When, on the following day, I met the proprietor of one of the oldest concerns in the Bowery,--which, while doing a legitimate business, caters necessarily to its crowds, and therefore sides with them,--he told me with bitter reproach how he had been stricken in pocket. A gambler had just been in to see him, who had come on from the far West, in anticipation of a wide-open town, and had got all ready to open a house in the Tenderloin. "He brought $40,000 to put in the business, and he came to take it away to Baltimore. Just now the cashier of ---- Bank told me that two other gentlemen--gamblers? yes, that's what you call them--had drawn $130,000 which they would have invested here, and had gone after him. Think of all that money gone to Baltimore! That's what you've done!"

I went over to police headquarters, thinking of the sad state of that man, and in the hallway I ran across two children, little tots, who were inquiring their way to "the commissioner." The older was a hunchback girl, who led her younger brother (he could not have been over five or six years old) by the hand. They explained their case to me. They came from Allen Street. Some undesirable women tenants had moved into the tenement, and when complaint was made that sent the police there, the children's father, who was a poor Jewish tailor, was blamed. The tenants took it out of the boy by punching his nose till it bled. Whereupon the children went straight to Mulberry Street to see the commissioner and get justice. It was the first time in twenty years that I had known Allen Street to come to police headquarters for justice; and in the discovery that the new idea had reached down to the little children I read the doom of the slum, despite its loud vauntings.

No, it was not true that reform was dead, with decency. It was not the slum that had won; it was we who had lost. We were not up to the mark,--not yet. But New York is a many times cleaner and better city to-day than it was ten years ago. Then I was able to grasp easily the whole plan for wresting it from the neglect and indifference that had put us where we were. It was chiefly, almost wholly, remedial in its scope. Now it is preventive, constructive, and no ten men could gather all the threads and hold them. We have made, are making headway, and no Tammany has the power to stop us. She knows it, too, and is in such frantic haste to fill her pockets while she has time that she has abandoned her old ally, the tax rate, and the pretense of making bad government cheap government. She is at this moment engaged in raising taxes and assessments at one and the same time to an unheard-of figure, while salaries are being increased lavishly on every hand. We can afford to pay all she charges us for the lesson we are learning. If to that we add common sense, we shall discover the bearings of it all without trouble. Yesterday I picked up a book,--a learned disquisition on government,--and read on the title-page, "Affectionately dedicated to all who despise politics." That was not common sense. To win the battle with the slum, we must not begin by despising politics. We have been doing that too long. The politics of the slum is apt to be like the slum itself, dirty. Then it must be cleaned. It is what the fight is about. Politics is the weapon. We must learn to use it so as to cut straight and sure. That is common sense, and the golden rule as applied to Tammany.

Some years ago, the United States government conducted an inquiry into the slums of great cities. To its staff of experts was attached a chemist, who gathered and isolated a lot of bacilli with fearsome Latin names, in the tenements where he went. Among those he labeled were the Staphylococcus pyogenes albus, the Micrococcus fervidosus, the Saccharomyces rosaceus, and the Bacillus buccalis fortuitus. I made a note of the names at the time, because of the dread with which they inspired me. But I searched the collection in vain for the real bacillus of the slum. It escaped science, to be identified by human sympathy and a conscience-stricken community with that of ordinary human selfishness. The antitoxin has been found, and is applied successfully. Since justice has replaced charity on the prescription the patient is improving. And the improvement is not confined to him; it is general. Conscience is not a local issue in our day. A few years ago, a United States Senator sought reelection on the platform that the decalogue and the golden rule were glittering generalities that had no place in politics, and lost. We have not quite reached the millennium yet, but to-day a man is governor in the Empire State who was elected on the pledge that he would rule by the ten commandments. These are facts that mean much or little, according to the way one looks at them. The significant thing is that they are facts, and that, in spite of slipping and sliding, the world moves forward, not backward. The poor we shall have always with us, but the slum we need not have. These two do not rightfully belong together. Their present partnership is at once poverty's worst hardship and our worst fault.

II

THE TENEMENT HOUSE BLIGHT

In a Stanton Street tenement, the other day, I stumbled upon a Polish capmaker's home. There were other capmakers in the house, Russian and Polish, but they simply "lived" there. This one had a home. The fact proclaimed itself the moment the door was opened, in spite of the darkness. The rooms were in the rear, gloomy with the twilight of the tenement, although the day was sunny without, but neat, even cosy. It was early, but the day's chores were evidently done. The teakettle sang on the stove, at which a bright-looking girl of twelve, with a pale but cheery face, and sleeves brushed back to the elbows, was busy poking up the fire. A little boy stood by the window, flattening his nose against the pane and gazing wistfully up among the chimney pots where a piece of blue sky about as big as the kitchen could be made out. I remarked to the mother that they were nice rooms.

"Ah yes," she said, with a weary little smile that struggled bravely with hope long deferred, "but it is hard to make a home here. We would so like to live in the front, but we can't pay the rent."

I knew the front with its unlovely view of the tenement street too well, and I said a good word for the air shaft--yard or court it could not be called, it was too small for that--which rather surprised myself. I had found few virtues enough in it before. The girl at the stove had left off poking the fire. She broke in the moment I finished, with eager enthusiasm: "Why, they have the sun in there. When the door is opened the light comes right in your face."

"Does it never come here?" I asked, and wished I had not done so, as soon as the words were spoken. The child at the window was listening, with his whole hungry little soul in his eyes.

Yes, it did, she said. Once every summer, for a little while, it came over the houses. She knew the month and the exact hour of the day when its rays shone into their home, and just the reach of its slant on the wall. They had lived there six years. In June the sun was due. A haunting fear that the baby would ask how long it was till June--it was February then--took possession of me, and I hastened to change the subject. Warsaw was their old home. They kept a little store there, and were young and happy. Oh, it was a fine city, with parks and squares, and bridges over the beautiful river,--and grass and flowers and birds and soldiers, put in the girl breathlessly. She remembered.

But the children kept coming, and they went across the sea to give them a better chance. Father made fifteen dollars a week, much money; but there were long seasons when there was no work. She, the mother, was never very well here,--she hadn't any strength; and the baby! She glanced at his grave white face, and took him in her arms. The picture of the two, and of the pale-faced girl longing back to the fields and the sunlight, in their prison of gloom and gray walls, haunts me yet. I have not had the courage to go back since. I recalled the report of an English army surgeon, which I read years ago, on the many more soldiers that died--were killed would be more correct--in barracks into which the sun never shone than in those that were open to the light.

The capmaker's case is the case of the nineteenth century, of civilization, against the metropolis of America. The home, the family, are the rallying points of civilization. But long since the tenements of New York earned for it the ominous name of "the homeless city." In its 40,000 tenements its workers, more than half of the city's population, are housed. They have no other chance. There are, indeed, wives and mothers who, by sheer force of character, rise above their environment and make homes where they go. Happily, there are yet many of them. But the fact remains that hitherto their struggle has been growing ever harder, and the issue more doubtful.

The tenement itself, with its crowds, its lack of privacy, is the greatest destroyer of individuality, of character. As its numbers increase, so does "the element that becomes criminal for lack of individuality and the self-respect that comes with it." Add the shiftless and the weak who are turned out by the same process, and you have its legitimate crop. In 1880 the average number of persons to each dwelling in New York was 16.37; in 1890 it was 18.52. In 1895, according to the police census, 21.2. The census of 1900 will show the crowding to have gone on at an equal if not at a greater rate. That will mean that so many more tenements have been built of the modern type, with four families to the floor where once there were two. I shall not weary the reader with many statistics. They are to be found, by those who want them, in the census books and in the official records. I shall try to draw from them their human story. But, as an instance of the unchecked drift, let me quote here the case of the Tenth Ward, that East Side district known as the most crowded in all the world. In 1880, when it had not yet attained that bad eminence, it contained 47,554 persons, or 432.3 to the acre. In 1890 the census showed a population of 57,596, which was 522 to the acre. The police census of 1895 found 70,168 persons living in 1514 houses, which was 643.08 to the acre. Lastly, the Health Department's census for the first half of 1898 gave a total of 82,175 persons living in 1201 tenements, with 313 inhabited buildings yet to be heard from. This is the process of doubling up,--literally, since the cause and the vehicle of it all is the double-decker tenement,-- which in the year 1895 had crowded a single block in that ward at the rate of 1526 persons per acre, and one in the Eleventh Ward at the rate of 1774.[1] It goes on not in the Tenth Ward or on the East Side only, but throughout the city. When, in 1897, it was proposed to lay out a small park in the Twenty-Second Ward, up on the far West Side, it was shown that five blocks in that section, between Forty-Ninth and Sixty-Second streets and Ninth and Eleventh avenues, had a population of more than 3000 each. The block between Sixty-First and Sixty-Second streets, Tenth and Eleventh avenues, harbored 3580, which meant 974.6 persons to the acre.

[Footnote 1: Police census of 1895: Block bounded by Canal, Hester, Eldridge, and Forsyth streets: size 375 ?200, population 2628, rate per acre 1526. Block bounded by Stanton, Houston, Attorney, and Ridge streets: size 200 ?300, population 2244, rate per acre 1774.]

If we have here to do with forces that are beyond the control of the individual or the community, we shall do well at least to face the facts squarely and know the truth. It is no answer to the charge that New York's way of housing its workers is the worst in the world to say that they are better off than they were where they came from. It is not true, in most cases, as far as the home is concerned: a shanty is better than a flat in a cheap tenement, any day. Even if it were true, it would still be beside the issue. In Poland my capmaker counted for nothing. Nothing was expected of him. Here he ranks, after a few brief years, politically equal with the man who hires his labor. A citizen's duty is expected of him, and home and citizenship are convertible terms. The observation of the Frenchman who had watched the experiment of herding two thousand human beings in eight tenement barracks in Paris, that the result was the "exasperation of the tenant against society," is true the world over. We have done as badly in New York. Social hatefulness is not a good soil for citizenship to grow in, where political equality rules.

Nor will the old lie about the tenants being wholly to blame cover the ground. It has long been overworked in defense of landlord usury. Doubtless there are bad tenants. In the matter of renting houses, as in everything else, men have a trick of coming up to what is expected of them, good or bad; but as a class the tenants have been shown all along to be superior to their surroundings. "Better than the houses they live in," said the first Tenement House Commission; and the second gave as its verdict that "they respond quickly to improved conditions." That is not an honest answer. The truth is that if we cannot check the indraught to the cities, we can, if we choose, make homes for those who come, and at a profit on the investment. Nothing has been more clearly demonstrated in our day, and it is time that it should be said so that everybody can understand. It is not a case of transforming human nature in the tenant, but of reforming it in the landlord builder. It is a plain question of the per cent. he is willing to take.

So that we may get the capmaker's view and that of his fellow tenants,--for, after all, that is the one that counts; the state and the community are not nearly so much interested in the profits of the landlord as in the welfare of the workers,--suppose we take a stroll through a tenement house neighborhood and see for ourselves. We were in Stanton Street. Let us start there, then, going east. Towering barracks on either side, five, six stories high. Teeming crowds. Push-cart men "moved on" by the policeman, who seems to exist only for the purpose. Forsyth Street: there is a church on the corner, Polish and Catholic, a combination that strikes one as queer here on the East Side, where Polish has come to be synonymous with Jewish. I have cause to remember that corner. A man killed his wife in this house, and was hanged for it. Just across the street, on the stoop of that brown stone tenement, the tragedy was re 韃 acted the next year; only the murderer saved the county trouble and expense by taking himself off, also. That other stoop in the same row witnessed a suicide. Why do I tell you these things? Because they are true. The policeman here will bear me out. They belong to the ordinary setting of life in a crowd such as this. It is never so little worth living, and therefore held so cheap along with the fierce, unceasing battle that goes on to save it. You will go no further unless I leave it out? Very well; I shall leave out the murder after we have passed the block yonder. The tragedy of that is of a kind that comes too close to the every-day life of tenement house people to be omitted. The house caught fire in the night, and five were burned to death,--father, mother, and three children. The others got out; why not they? They stayed, it seems, to make sure none was left; they were not willing to leave one behind, to save themselves. And then it was too late; the stairs were burning. There was no proper fire escape. That was where the murder came in; but it was not all chargeable to the landlord, nor even the greater part. More than thirty years ago, in 1867, the state made it law that the stairs in every tenement four stories high should be fireproof, and forbade the storing of any inflammable material in such houses. I do not know when the law was repealed, or if it ever was. I only know that in 1892 the Fire Department, out of pity for the tenants and regard for the safety of its own men, forced through an amendment to the building law, requiring the stairs of the common type of five-story tenements to be built of fireproof material, and that to-day they are of wood, just as they always were. Only last spring I looked up the Superintendent of Buildings and asked him what it meant. I showed him the law, which said that the stairs should be "built of slow-burning construction or fireproof material;" and he put his finger upon the clause that follows, "as the Superintendent of Buildings shall decide." The law gave him discretion, and that is how he used it. "Hard wood burns slowly," said he.

The fire of which I speak was a "cruller fire," if I remember rightly, which is to say that it broke out in the basement bakeshop, where they were boiling crullers (doughnuts) in fat, at four A. M., with a hundred tenants asleep in the house above them. The fat went into the fire, and the rest followed. I suppose that I had to do with a hundred such fires, as a police reporter, before, under the protest of the Tenement House Committee and the Good Government Clubs, the boiling of fat in tenement bakeshops was forbidden. The chief of the Fire Department, in his testimony before the committee, said that "tenements are erected mainly with a view of returning a large income for the amount of capital invested. It is only after a fire in which great loss of life occurs that any interest whatever is taken in the safety of the occupants." The Superintendent of Buildings, after such a fire in March, 1896, said that there were thousands of tenement fire-traps in the city. My reporter's notebook bears witness to the correctness of his statement, and it has many blank leaves that are waiting to be put to that use yet. The reckoning for eleven years showed that, of 35,844 fires in New York, 53.18 per cent. were in tenement houses, though they were only a little more than 31 per cent. of all the buildings, and that 177 occupants were killed, 523 maimed, and 625 rescued by the firemen. Their rescue cost the lives of three of these brave men, and 453 were injured in the effort. And when all that is said, not the half is told. A fire in the night in one of those human beehives, with its terror and woe, is one of the things that live in the recollection ever after as a terrible nightmare. Yet the demonstration of the Tenement House Committee, that to build tenements fireproof from the ground up would cost little over ten per cent. more than is spent upon the firetrap, and would more than return the interest on the extra outlay in the saving of insurance and repairs, and in the better building every way, has found no echo in legislation or in the practice of builders. That was the fire chief's way to avoid "the great destruction of life;" but he warned the committee that it would "meet with strong opposition from the different interests, should legislation be requested." The interest of the man who pays the rent will not be suspected in this, so he must have meant the man who collects it.

Here is a block of tenements inhabited by poor Jews. Most of the Jews who live over here are poor; and the poorer they are, the higher rent do they pay, and the more do they crowd to make it up between them. "The destruction of the poor is their poverty." It is only the old story in a new setting. The slum landlord's profits were always the highest. He spends nothing for repairs, and lays the blame on the tenant. The "district leader" saves him, in these days of Tammany rule come back, unless he is on the wrong side of the political fence, in which case the Sanitary Code comes handy to chase him into camp. A big "order" on his house is a very effective way of making a tenement house landlord discern political truth on the eve of an important election. Just before the last, when the election of Theodore Roosevelt was threatened, the sanitary force displayed such activity as it has not since, up to the raid on the elevated roads, in the examination of tenements belonging very largely, as it happened, to sympathizers with the gallant Rough Rider's cause; and those who knew did not marvel much at the large vote polled by the Tammany candidate in the old city.

The halls of these tenements are dark. Under the law, there should be a light burning, but it is one of the rarest things to find one. The thing seems well-nigh impossible of accomplishment. Two years ago, when the Good Government Clubs set about backing up the Board of Health in its efforts to work out this reform, which comes close to being one of the most necessary of all,--such untold mischief is abroad in the darkness of these thoroughfares,--the sanitary police reported 12,000 tenement halls unlighted by night, even, and brought them, by repeated orders, down to less than

1000 in six months. I do not believe the light burns in 1000 of them all to-day. It is so easy to put it out when the policeman's back is turned, and save the gas.

We had a curious instance at the time of the difficulties that sometimes beset reform. Certain halls that were known to be dark were reported sufficiently lighted by the policeman of the district, and it was discovered that it was his standard that was vitiated. He himself lived in a tenement, and was used to its gloom. So an order was issued defining darkness to the sanitary police: if the sink in the hall could be made out, and the slops overflowing on the floor, and if a baby could be seen on the stairs, the hall was light; if, on the other hand, the baby's shrieks were the first warning that it was being trampled upon, the hall was dark. Some days later, the old question arose about an Eldridge Street tenement. The policeman had reported the hall light enough. The president of the Board of Health, to settle it once for all, went over with me, to see for himself. The hall was very dark. He sent for the policeman.

"Did you see the sink in that hall?" he asked.

The policeman said he did.

"But it is pitch dark. How did you see it?"

"I lit a match," said the policeman.

Four families live on these floors, with Heaven knows how many children. It was here the police commissioners were requested, in sober earnest, some years ago, by a committee of very practical women philanthropists, to have the children tagged, so as to save the policemen wear and tear in taking them back and forth between the Eldridge Street police station and headquarters, when they got lost. If tagged, they could be assorted at once and taken to their homes. Incidentally, the city would save the expense of many meals. It was shrewdly suspected that the little ones were lost on purpose in a good many cases, as a way of getting them fed at the public expense.

That the children preferred the excitement of the police station, and the distinction of a trip in charge of a brass-buttoned guardian, to the Ludlow

Street flat is easy enough to understand. A more unlovely existence than that in one of these tenements it would be hard to imagine. Everywhere is the stench of the kerosene stove that is forever burning, serving for cooking, heating, and ironing alike, until the last atom of oxygen is burned out of the close air. Oil is cheaper than coal. The air shaft is too busy carrying up smells from below to bring any air down, even if it is not hung full of washing in every story, as it ordinarily is. Enterprising tenants turn it to use as a refrigerator as well. There is at least a draught of air, such as it is. When fire breaks out, this draught makes of the air shaft a flue through which the fire roars fiercely to the roof, so transforming what was meant for the good of the tenants into their greatest peril. The stuffy rooms seem as if they were made for dwarfs. Most decidedly, there is not room to swing the proverbial cat in any one of them. In one I helped the children, last holiday, to set up a Christmas tree, so that a glimpse of something that was not utterly sordid and mean might for once enter their lives. Three weeks after, I found the tree standing yet in the corner. It was very cold, and there was no fire in the room. "We were going to burn it," said the little woman, whose husband was then in the insane asylum, "and then I couldn't. It looked so kind o' cheery-like there in the corner." My tree had borne the fruit I wished.

It remained for the New York slum landlord to assess the exact value of a ray of sunlight,--upon the tenant, of course. Here are two back-to-back rear tenements, with dark bedrooms on the south. The flat on the north gives upon a neighbor's yard, and a hole two feet square has been knocked in the wall, letting in air and sunlight; little enough of the latter, but what there is is carefully computed in the lease. Six dollars for this flat, six and a half for the one with the hole in the wall. Six dollars a year per ray. In half a dozen houses in this block have I found the same rate maintained. The modern tenement on the corner goes higher: for four front rooms, "where the sun comes right in your face," seventeen dollars; for the rear flat of three rooms, larger and better every other way, but always dark, like the capmaker's, eleven dollars. From the landlord's point of view, this last is probably a concession. But he is a landlord with a heart. His house is as good a one as can be built on a twenty-five-foot lot. The man who owns the corner building in Orchard Street, with the two adjoining tenements, has no heart. In the depth of last winter, I found a family of poor Jews living in a coop under his stairs, an abandoned piece of hallway, in which their baby was born, and for which he made them pay eight dollars a month. It was the most outrageous case of landlord robbery I had ever come across, and it gave me sincere pleasure to assist the sanitary policeman in curtailing his profits by even this much. The hall is not now occupied.

The Jews under the stairs had two children. The shoemaker in the cellar next door has three. They were fighting and snarling like so many dogs over the coarse food on the table before them, when we looked in. The baby, it seems, was the cause of the row. He wanted it all. He was a very dirty and a very fierce baby, and the other two children were no match for him. The shoemaker grunted fretfully at his last, "Ach, he is all de time hungry!" At the sight of the policeman, the young imp set up such a howl that we beat a hasty retreat. The cellar "flat" was undoubtedly in violation of law, but it was allowed to pass. In the main hall, on the ground floor, we counted seventeen children. The facts of life here suspend ordinary landlord prejudices to a certain extent. Occasionally it is the tenant who suspends them. The policeman laughed as he told me of the case of a mother who coveted a flat into which she well knew her family would not be admitted; the landlord was particular. She knocked, with a troubled face, alone. Yes, the flat was to let; had she any children? The woman heaved a sigh. "Six, but they are all in Greenwood." The landlord's heart was touched by such woe. He let her have the flat. By night he was amazed to find a flock of half a dozen robust youngsters domiciled under his roof. They had indeed been in Greenwood; but they had come back from the cemetery to stay. And stay they did, the rent being paid.

High rents, slack work, and low wages go hand in hand in the tenements as promoters of overcrowding. The rent is always one fourth of the family income, often more. The fierce competition for a bare living cuts down wages; and when loss of work is added, the only thing left is to take in lodgers to meet the landlord's claim. The Jew usually takes them singly, the Italian by families. The midnight visit of the sanitary policeman discloses a state of affairs against which he feels himself helpless. He has his standard: 400 cubic feet of air space for each adult sleeper, 200 for a child. That in itself is a concession to the practical necessities of the case. The original demand was for 600 feet. But of 28,000 and odd tenants canvassed in New York, in the slumming investigation prosecuted by the general government in 1894, 17,047 were found to have less than 400 feet, and of these 5526 slept in unventilated rooms with no windows. No more such rooms have been added since; but there has come that which is worse.

It was the boast of New York, till a few years ago, that at least that worst of tenement depravities, the one-room house, too familiar in the English slums, was practically unknown here. It is not so any longer. The evil began in the old houses in Orchard and Allen streets, a bad neighborhood, infested by fallen women and the thievish rascals who prey upon their misery,--a region where the whole plan of humanity, if plan there be in this disgusting mess, jars out of tune continually. The furnished-room house has become an institution here, speeded on by a conscienceless Jew who bought up the old buildings as fast as they came into the market, and filled them with a class of tenants before whom charity recoils, helpless and hopeless. When the houses were filled, the crowds overflowed into the yard. In one case, I found, in midwinter, tenants living in sheds built of odd boards and roof tin, and paying a dollar a week for herding with the rats. One of them, a red-faced German, was a philosopher after his kind. He did not trouble himself to get up, when I looked in, but stretched himself in his bed,--it was high noon,--responding to my sniff of disgust that it was "sehr schoen! ein bischen kalt, aber was!" His neighbor, a white-haired old woman, begged, trembling, not to be put out. She would not know where to go. It was out of one of these houses that Fritz Meyer, the murderer, went to rob the poorbox in the Redemptorist Church, the night when he killed policeman Smith. The policeman surprised him at his work. In the room he had occupied I came upon a brazen-looking woman with a black eye, who answered the question of the officer, "Where did you get that shiner?" with a laugh. "I ran up against the fist of me man," she said. Her "man," a big, sullen lout, sat by, dumb. The woman answered for him that he was a mechanic.

"What does he work at?" snorted the policeman, restraining himself with an effort from kicking the fellow.

She laughed scornfully. "At the junk business." It meant that he was a thief.

Young men, with blotched faces and cadaverous looks, were loafing in every room. They hung their heads in silence. The women turned their faces away at the sight of the uniform. They cling to these wretches, who exploit their starved affections for their own ease, with a grip of desperation. It is their last hold. Women have to love something. It is their deepest degradation that they must love these. Even the wretches themselves feel the shame of it, and repay them by beating and robbing them, as their daily occupation. A poor little baby in one of the rooms gave a shuddering human touch to it all.

The old houses began it, as they began all the tenement mischief that has come upon New York. But the opportunity that was made by the tenant's need was not one to be neglected. In some of the newer tenements, with their smaller rooms, the lodger is by this time provided for in the plan, with a special entrance from the hall. "Lodger" comes, by an easy transition, to stand for "family." Only the other night I went with the sanitary police on their midnight inspection through a row of Elizabeth Street tenements which I had known since they were built, fifteen or sixteen years ago. That is the neighborhood in which the recent Italian immigrants crowd. In the house which we selected for examination, in all respects the type of the rest, we found forty-three families where there should have been sixteen. Upon each floor were four flats, and in each flat three rooms that measured respectively 14 x 11, 7 x 11, and 7 x 8-1/2 feet. In only one flat did we find a single family. In three there were two to each. In the other twelve each room had its own family living and sleeping there. They cooked, I suppose, at the one stove in the kitchen, which was the largest room. In one big bed we counted six persons, the parents and four children. Two of them lay crosswise at the foot of the bed, or there would not have been room. A curtain was hung before the bed in each of the two smaller rooms, leaving a passageway from the hall to the main room. The rent for the front flats was twelve dollars; for that in the rear ten dollars. The social distinctions going with the advantage of location were rigidly observed, I suppose. The three steps across a tenement hall, from the front to "the back," are often a longer road than from Ludlow Street to Fifth Avenue.

They were sweaters' tenements. But I shall keep that end of the story until I come to speak of the tenants. The houses I have in mind now. They were Astor leasehold property, and I had seen them built upon the improved plan of 1879, with air shafts and all that. There had not been water in the tenements for a month then, we were told by the one tenant who spoke English that could be understood. The cold snap had locked the pipes. Fitly enough, the lessee was an undertaker, an Italian himself, who combined with his business of housing his people above and below the ground that of the padrone, to let no profit slip. He had not taken the trouble to make many or recent repairs. The buildings had made a fair start; they promised well. But the promise had not been kept. In their premature decay they were distinctly as bad as the worst. I had the curiosity to seek out the agent, the middleman, and ask him why they were so. He shrugged his shoulders. With such tenants nothing could be done, he said. I have always held that Italians are most manageable, and that, with all the surface indications to the contrary, they are really inclined to cleanliness, if cause can be shown, and I told him so. He changed the subject diplomatically. No doubt it was with him simply a question of the rent. They might crowd and carry on as they pleased, once that was paid; and they did. It used to be the joke of Elizabeth Street that when the midnight police came, the tenants would keep them waiting outside, pretending to search for the key, until the surplus population of men had time to climb down the fire escape. When the police were gone they came back. We surprised them all in bed.

Like most of the other tenements we have come across on our trip, these were double-deckers. That is the type of tenement that is responsible for the crowding that goes on unchecked. It is everywhere replacing the older barracks, as they rot or are torn down.

This double-decker was thus described by the Tenement House Committee of 1894: "It is the one hopeless form of tenement construction. It cannot be well ventilated, it cannot be well lighted; it is not safe in case of fire. It is built on a lot 25 feet wide by 100 or less in depth, with apartments for four families in each story. This necessitates the occupation of from 86 to 90 per cent. of the lot's depth. The stairway, made in the centre of the house, and the necessary walls and partitions reduce the width of the middle rooms (which serve as bedrooms for at least two people each) to 9 feet each at the most, and a narrow light and air shaft, now legally required in the centre of each side wall, still further lessens the floor space of these middle rooms. Direct light is only possible for the rooms at the front and rear. The middle rooms must borrow what light they can from dark hallways, the shallow shafts, and the rear rooms. Their air must pass through other rooms or the tiny shafts, and cannot but be contaminated before it reaches them. A five-story house of this character contains apartments for eighteen or twenty families, a population frequently amounting to 100 people, and sometimes increased by boarders or lodgers to 150 or more."

The committee, after looking in vain through the slums of the Old World cities for something to compare the double-deckers with, declared that, in their setting, the separateness and sacredness of home life were interfered with, and evils bred, physical and moral, that "conduce to the corruption of the young." The statement needs no argument to convince.

Yet it is for these that the "interests" of which the fire chief spoke rush into battle at almost every session of the legislature, whenever a step, no matter how short and conservative, is to be taken toward their improvement. No winter has passed, since the awakening conscience of the people of New York city manifested itself in a desire to better the lot of the other half, that has not seen an assault made, in one shape or another, on the structure of tenement house law built up with such anxious solicitude. Once a bill to exempt from police supervision, by withdrawing them from the tenement house class, the very worst of the houses, whose death rate threatened the community, was sneaked through the legislature all unknown, and had reached the executive before the alarm was sounded. The governor, put upon his guard, returned the bill, with the indorsement that he was unable to understand what could have prompted a measure that seemed to have reason and every argument against it, and none for it. But the motive is not so obscure, after all. It is the same old one of profit without conscience. It took from the Health Department the supervision of the light, ventilation, and plumbing of the tenements, which by right belonged there, and put it in charge of a compliant Building Department, "for the convenience of architects and their clients, and the saving of time and expense to them." For the convenience of the architect's client, the builder, the lot was encroached upon, until of one big block which the Tenement House Committee measured only 7 per cent. was left uncovered for the air to struggle through; 93 per cent. of it was covered with brick and mortar. Rear tenements, to the number of nearly 100, have been condemned as "slaughter houses," with good reason, but this block was built practically solid. The average of space covered in 34 tenement blocks was shown to be 78.13 per cent. The law allowed only 65. The "discretion" that pens tenants in a burning tenement with stairs of wood for the builder's "convenience" cut down the chance of life of their babies unmoved. Sunlight and air mean just that, where three thousand human beings are packed into a single block. That was why the matter was given into the charge of the health officials, when politics was yet kept out of their work.

Of such kind are the interests that oppose betterment of the worker's hard lot in New York; that dictated the appointment by Tammany of a commission composed of builders to revise its code of building laws, and that sneer at the "laughable results of the late Tenement House Committee." Those results made for the health and happiness and safety of a million and a half of souls, and were accounted, on every humane ground, the longest step forward that had yet been taken by this community. For the old absentee landlord, who did not know what mischief was afoot, we have got the speculative builder, who does know, but does not care so long as he gets his pound of flesh. Half of the just laws that have been passed for the relief of the people he has paralyzed with his treacherous discretion clause, carefully nursed in the school of practical politics to which he gives faithful adherence. The thing has been the curse of our city from the day when the earliest struggle toward better things began. Among the first manifestations of that was the prohibition of soap factories below Grand Street by the act of 1797, which created a Board of Health with police powers. The act was passed in February, to take effect in July; but long before that time the same legislature had amended it by giving the authorities discretion in the matter. And the biggest soap factory of them all is down there to this day, and is even now stirring up a rumpus among the latest immigrants, the Syrians, who have settled about it. No doubt it is all a question of political education; but are not a hundred years enough to settle this much, that compromise is out of place where the lives of the people are at stake, and that it is time our years of "discretion" were numbered?

And, please God, the time is at hand. Here, set in its frame of swarming tenements, is a wide open space, some time, when enough official red tape has been unwound, to be a park, with flowers and grass and birds to gladden the hearts of those to whom such things have been as tales that are told, all these dreary years, and with a playground in which the children of yonder big school may roam at will, undismayed by landlord or policeman. Not all the forces of reaction can put back the barracks that were torn down as one of the "laughable results" of that very Tenement House Committee's work, or restore to the undertaker his profits from Bone Alley of horrid memory. It was the tenant's turn to laugh, that time. Down half a dozen blocks, among even denser swarms, is another such plot, where football and a skating pond are being planned by the children's friends. We shall hear the story of these yet, and rejoice that the day of reckoning is coming for the builder without a soul. Till then let him deck the fronts of his tenements with bravery of plate glass and brass to hide the darkness within. He has done his worst.

We can go no further. Yonder lies the river. A full mile we have come, through unbroken ranks of tenements with their mighty, pent-up multitudes. Here they seem, with a common impulse, to overflow into the street. From corner to corner it is crowded with girls and children dragging babies nearly as big as themselves, with desperate endeavor to lose nothing of the show. There is a funeral in the block. Unnumbered sewing-machines cease for once their tireless rivalry with the flour mill in the next block, that is forever grinding in a vain effort to catch up. Heads are poked from windows. On the stoops hooded and shawled figures have front seats. The crowd is hardly restrained by the policeman and the undertaker in holiday mourning, who clear a path by force to the plumed hearse. The eager haste, the frantic rush to see,--what does it not tell of these starved lives, of the quality of their aims and ambitions? The mill clatters loudly: there is one mouth less to fill. In the midst of it all, with clamor of urgent gong, the patrol wagon rounds the corner, carrying two policemen precariously perched upon a struggling "drunk," a woman. The crowd scatters, following the new sensation. The tragedies of death and life in the slum have met together.

Many a mile I might lead you along these rivers, east and west, through the island of Manhattan, and find little else than we have seen. The great crowd is yet below Fourteenth Street, but the northward march knows no slackening of pace. As the tide sets uptown, it reproduces faithfully the scenes of the older wards, though with less of their human interest than here where the old houses, in all their ugliness, have yet some imprint of the individuality of their tenants. Only on feast days does Little Italy, in Harlem, recall the Bend when it put on holiday attire. Anything more desolate and disheartening than the unending rows of tenements, all alike and all equally repellent, of the uptown streets, it is hard to imagine. Hell's Kitchen in its ancient wickedness was picturesque, at least, with its rocks and its goats and shanties. Since the negroes took possession it is only dull, except when, as happened last summer, the remnant of the Irish settlers make a stand against the intruders. Vain hope! Perpetual eviction is their destiny. Negro, Italian, and Jew, biting the dust with many a bruised head under the Hibernian's stalwart fist, resistlessly drive him before them, nevertheless, out of house and home. The landlord pockets the gate money. The old robbery still goes on. Where the negro pitches his tent, he pays more rent than his white neighbor next door, and is a better tenant. And he is good game forever. He never buys the tenement, as the Jew or the Italian is likely to do, when he has scraped up money enough to re 韮 act, after his own fashion, the trick taught him by his oppressor. The black column has reached the hundredth street on the East Side, and the sixties on the West,[2] and there for the present it halts. Jammed between Africa, Italy, and Bohemia, the Irishman has abandoned the East Side uptown. Only west of Central Park does he yet face his foe, undaunted in defeat as in victory. The local street nomenclature, in which the directory has no hand,--Nigger Row, Mixed Ale Flats, etc.,--indicates the hostile camps with unerring accuracy.

[Footnote 2: There is an advanced outpost of blacks as far up as One Hundred and Forty-Fifth Street, but the main body lingers yet among the sixties.]

Uptown or downtown, as the tenements grow taller, the thing that is rarest to find is the home of the olden days, even as it was in the shanty on the rocks. "No home, no family, no morality, no manhood, no patriotism!" said the old Frenchman. Seventy-seven per cent. of their young prisoners, say the managers of the state reformatory, have no moral sense, or next to none. "Weakness, not wickedness, ails them," adds the prison chaplain; no manhood, that is to say. Years ago, roaming through the British Museum, I came upon an exhibit that riveted my attention as nothing else had. It was a huge stone arm, torn from the shoulder of some rock image, with doubled fist and every rigid muscle instinct with angry menace. Where it came from or what was its story I do not know. I did not ask. It was its message to us I was trying to read. I had been spending weary days and nights in the slums of London, where hatred grew, a noxious crop, upon the wreck of the home. Lying there, mute and menacing, the great fist seemed to me like a shadow thrown from the gray dawn of the race into our busy day with a purpose, a grim, unheeded warning. What was it? In the slum the question haunts me yet. They perished, the empires those rock-hewers built, and the governments reared upon their ruins are long since dead and forgotten. They were born to die, for they were not built upon human happiness, but upon human terror and greed. We built ours upon the bed rock, and its cornerstone is the home. With this bitter mockery of it that makes the slum, can it be that the warning is indeed for us?

THE TENEMENT: CURING ITS BLIGHT

I stood at Seven Dials and heard the policeman's account of what it used to be. Seven Dials is no more like the slum of old than is the Five Points to-day. The conscience of London wrought upon the one as the conscience of New York upon the other. A mission house, a children's refuge, two big schools, and, hard by, a public bath and a wash house stand as the record of the battle with the slum, which, with these forces in the field, has but one ending. The policeman's story rambled among the days when things were different. Then it was dangerous for an officer to go alone there at night.

Around the corner there came from one of the side streets a procession with banners, parading in honor and aid of some church charity. We watched it pass. In it marched young men and boys with swords and battle-axes, and upon its outskirts skipped a host of young roughs--so one would have called them but for the evidence of their honest employment--who rattled collection boxes, reaping a harvest of pennies from far and near. I looked at the battle-axes and the collection boxes, and thought of forty years ago. Where were the Seven Dials of that day, and the men who gave it its bad name? I asked the policeman.

"They were druv into decency, sor," he said, and answered from his own experience the question ever asked by faint-hearted philanthropists. "My father, he done duty here afore me in '45. The worst dive was where that church stands. It was always full of thieves,"--whose sons, I added mentally, have become collectors for the church. The one fact was a whole chapter on the slum.

London's way with the tenant we adopted at last in New York with the slum landlord. He was "druv into decency." We had to. Moral suasion had been stretched to the limit. The point had been reached where one knock-down blow outweighed a bushel of arguments. It was all very well to build model tenements as object lessons to show that the thing could be done; it had become necessary to enforce the lesson by demonstrating that the community had power to destroy houses which were a menace to its life. The rear tenements were chosen for this purpose.

They were the worst as they were the first of New York's tenements. The double-deckers of which I have spoken had, with all their evils, at least this to their credit, that their death rate was not nearly as high as that of the old houses. That was not because of any virtue inherent in the double-deckers, but because the earlier tenements were old, and built in a day that knew nothing of sanitary restrictions, and cared less. Hence the showing that the big tenements had much the lowest mortality. The death rate does not sound the depths of tenement house evils, but it makes a record that is needed when it comes to attacking property rights. The mortality of the rear tenements had long been a scandal. They are built in the back yard, generally back to back with the rear buildings on abutting lots. If there is an open space between them, it is never more than a slit a foot or so wide, and gets to be the receptacle of garbage and filth of every kind; so that any opening made in these walls for purposes of ventilation becomes a source of greater danger than if there were none. The last count that was made, in 1898, showed that among the 40,958 tenements in New York there were still 2379 rear houses left. Where they are the death rate rises, for reasons that are apparent. The sun cannot reach them. They are damp and dark, and the tenants, who are always the poorest and most crowded, live "as in a cage open only toward the front," said the Tenement House Committee. A canvass made of the mortality records by Dr. Roger S. Tracy, the registrar of records, showed that while in the First Ward (the oldest), for instance, the death rate in houses standing singly on the lot was 29.03 per 1000 of the living, where there were rear houses it rose to 61.97. The infant death rate is a still better test: that rose from 109.58 in the single tenements of the same ward to 204.54 where there were rear houses. One in every five babies had to die, that is to say; the house killed it. No wonder the committee styled the rear tenements "slaughter houses," and called upon the legislature to root them out, and with them every old, ramshackle, disease-breeding tenement in the city.

A law which is in substance a copy of the English act for destroying slum property was passed in the spring of 1895. It provides for the seizure of buildings that are dangerous to the public health or unfit for human habitation, and their destruction upon proper proof, with compensation to the owner on a sliding scale down to the point of entire unfitness, when he is entitled only to the value of the material in his house. Up to that time, the only way to get rid of such a house had been to declare it a nuisance under the sanitary code; but as the city could not very well pay for the removal of a nuisance, to order it down seemed too much like robbery; so the owner was allowed to keep it. It takes time and a good many lives to grow a sentiment such as this law expressed. The Anglo-Saxon respect for vested rights is strong in us, also. I remember going through a ragged school in London, once, and finding the eyes of the children in the infant class red and sore. Suspecting some contagion, I made inquiries, and was told that a collar factory next door was the cause of the trouble. The fumes from it poisoned the children's eyes.

"And you allow it to stay, and let this thing go on?" I asked, in wonder.

The superintendent shrugged his shoulders. "It is their factory," he said.

I was on the point of saying something that might not have been polite, seeing that I was a guest, when I remembered that, in the newspaper which I carried in my pocket, I had just been reading a plea of some honorable M. P. for a much-needed reform in the system of counsel fees, then being agitated in the House of Commons. The reply of the solicitor general had made me laugh. He was inclined to agree with the honorable member, but still preferred to follow precedent by referring the matter to the Inns of Court. Quite incidentally, he mentioned that the matter had been hanging fire in the House two hundred years. It seemed very English to me then; but when we afterward came to tackle our rear tenements, and in the first batch there was a row which I knew to have been picked out by the sanitary inspector, twenty-five years before, as fit only to be destroyed, I recognized that we were kin, after all.

That was Gotham Court. It was first on the list, and the Mott Street Barracks came next, when, as executive officer of the Good Government Clubs, I helped the Board of Health put the law to the test the following year. The Health Department kept a list of 66 old houses, with a population of 5460 tenants, in which there had been 1313 deaths in a little over five years (1889-94). From among them we picked our lot, and the department drove the tenants out. The owners went to law, one and all; but, to their surprise and dismay, the courts held with the health officers. The moral effect was instant and overwhelming. Rather than keep up the fight, with no rent coming in, the landlords surrendered at discretion. In consideration of this, compensation was allowed them at the rate of about a thousand dollars a house, although they were really entitled only to the value of the old material. The buildings all came under the head of "wholly unfit." Gotham Court, with its sixteen buildings, in which, thirty-five years ago, a health inspector counted 146 cases of sickness, including "all kinds of infectious disease," was bought for $19,750, and Mullen's Court, adjoining, for $7251. They had been under civilized management since, but nothing decent could be made out of them. To show the character of all, let two serve; in each case it is the official record, upon which seizure was made, that is quoted:--

No. 98 Catherine Street: "The floor in the apartments and the wooden steps leading to the second-floor apartment are broken, loose, saturated with filth. The roof and eaves gutters leak, rendering the apartments wet. The two apartments on the first floor consist of one room each, in which the tenants are compelled to cook, eat, and sleep. The back walls are defective; the house wet and damp, and unfit for human habitation. It robs the surrounding houses of light."

"The sunlight never enters" was the constant refrain.

No. 17 Sullivan Street: "Occupied by the lowest whites and negroes, living together. The houses are decayed from cellar to garret, and filthy beyond description,--the filthiest, in fact, we have ever seen. The beams, the floors, the plaster on the walls, where there is any plaster, are rotten and alive with vermin. They are a menace to the public health, and cannot be repaired. Their annual death rate in five years was 41.38."

The sunlight enters where these stood, at all events, and into 58 other yards that once were plague spots. Of 94 rear tenements seized that year, 60 have been torn down, 33 of them voluntarily by the owners; 29 were remodeled and allowed to stand, chiefly as workshops; 5 other houses were standing empty, and yielding no rent, in March, 1899. The worst of them all, the Mott Street Barracks, are yet in the courts; but all the judges and juries in the land have no power to put them back. It is a case of "They can't put you in jail for that"--"Yes, but I am in jail." They are gone, torn down under the referee's decision that they ought to go, before the Appellate Division called a halt. In 1888 I counted 360 tenants in these tenements, front and rear, all Italians, and the infant death rate of the Barracks that year was 325 per 1000. There were forty babies, and one in three of them had to die. The general infant death rate for the whole tenement house population that year was 88.38. In the four years following, during which the population and the death rate of the houses were both reduced with an effort, fifty-one funerals went out of the Barracks. With entire fitness, a cemetery corporation held the mortgage upon the property. The referee allowed it the price of opening one grave, in the settlement, gave one dollar to the lessee and one hundred and ten dollars to the landlord, who refused to collect, and took his case to the Court of Appeals, where it is to be argued this summer. The only interest that attaches to it, since the real question has been decided by the wrecker ahead of time, is the raising of the constitutional point, perchance, and the issue of that is not doubtful. The law has been repeatedly upheld, and in Massachusetts, where similar action has been taken since, the constitutionality of it has in no case been attacked, so far as I know.

I have said before that I do not believe in paying the slum landlord for taking his hand off our throats, when we have got the grip on him in turn. Mr. Roger Foster, who as a member of the Tenement House Committee drew the law, and as counsel for the Health Department fought the landlords successfully in the courts, holds to the opposite view. I am bound to say that instances turned up in which it did seem a hardship to deprive the owners of even such property. I remember especially a tenement in Roosevelt Street, which was the patrimony and whole estate of two children. With the rear house taken away, the income from the front would not be enough to cover the interest on the mortgage. It was one of those things that occasionally make standing upon abstract principle so very uncomfortable. I confess I never had the courage to ask what was done in their case. I know that the tenement went, and I hope--Well, never mind what I hope. It has nothing to do with the case. The house is down, and the main issue decided upon its merits.

In the 94 tenements (counting the front houses in; they cannot be separated from the rear tenements in the death registry) there were in five years 956 deaths, a rate of 62.9 at a time when the general city death rate was 24.63. It was the last and heaviest blow aimed at the abnormal mortality of a city that ought, by reason of many advantages, to be one of the healthiest in the world. With clean streets, pure milk, medical school inspection, antitoxin treatment of deadly diseases, and better sanitary methods generally; with the sunlight let into its slums, and its worst plague spots cleaned out, the death rate of New York came down from 26.32 per 1000 inhabitants in 1887 to 19.53 in 1897. Inasmuch as a round half million was added to its population within the ten years, it requires little figuring to show that the number whose lives were literally saved by reform would people a city of no mean proportions. The extraordinary spell of hot weather, two years ago, brought out the full meaning of this. While many were killed by sunstroke, the population as a whole was shown to have acquired, in better hygienic surroundings, a much greater power of resistance. It yielded slowly to the heat. Where two days had been sufficient, in former years, to send the death rate up, it now took five; and the infant mortality remained low throughout the dreadful trial. Perhaps the substitution of beer for whiskey as a summer drink had something to do with it; but Colonel Waring's broom and unpolitical sanitation had more. Since it spared him so many voters, the politician ought to have been grateful for this; but he was not. Death rates are not as good political arguments as tax rates, we found out. In the midst of it all, a policeman whom I knew went to his Tammany captain to ask if Good Government Clubs were political clubs within the meaning of the law, which prohibits policemen from joining such. The answer he received set me to thinking: "Yes, the meanest, worst kind of political clubs, they are." Yet they had done nothing worse than to save the babies, the captain's with the rest.

The landlord read the signs better. He learned his lesson quickly. All over the city, he made haste to set his house to rights, lest it be seized or brought to the bar in other ways. The Good Government Clubs did not rest content with their first victory. They made war upon the dark hall in the double-decker, and upon the cruller bakery. They opened small parks, exposed the abuses of the civil courts, the "poor man's courts," urged on the building of new schools, compelled the cleaning of the Tombs prison and hastened the demolition of the wicked old pile, and took a hand in evolving a sensible and humane system of dealing with the young vagrants who were going to waste on free soup. The proposition to establish a farm colony for their reclamation was met with the challenge at Albany that "we have had enough reform in New York city," and, as the event proved, for the time being we had really gone as far as we could. But even that was a good long way. Some things had been nailed that could never again be undone; and hand in hand with the effort to destroy had gone another to build up, that promised to set us far enough ahead to appeal at last successfully to the self-interest of the builder, if not to his humanity; or, failing that, to compel him to decency. If that promise has not been kept, the end is not yet. I believe it will be kept.

The movement for reform, in the matter of housing the people, had proceeded upon a clearly outlined plan that apportioned to each of several forces its own share of the work. At a meeting held under the auspices of the Association for Improving the Condition of the Poor, early in the days of the movement, the field had been gone over thoroughly. To the Good Government Clubs fell the task, as already set forth, of compelling the enforcement of the existing tenement house laws. D. O. Mills, the philanthropic banker, declared his purpose to build hotels which should prove that a bed and lodging as good as any could be furnished to the great army of homeless men at a price that would compete with the cheap lodging houses, and yet yield a profit to the owner. On behalf of a number of well-known capitalists, who had been identified with the cause of tenement house reform for years, Robert Fulton Cutting, the president of the Association for Improving the Condition of the Poor, offered to build homes for the working people that should be worthy of the name, on a large scale. A company was formed, and chose for its president Dr. Elgin R. L. Gould, author of the government report on the Housing of the Working People, the standard work on the subject. A million dollars were raised by public subscription, and operations were begun at once.

Two ideas were kept in mind as fundamental: one, that charity that will not pay will not stay; the other, that nothing can be done with the twenty-five-foot lot. It is the primal curse of our housing system, and any effort toward better things must reckon with it first. Nineteen lots on Sixty-Eighth and Sixty-Ninth streets, west of Tenth Avenue, were purchased of Mrs. Alfred Corning Clark, who took one tenth of the capital stock of the City and Suburban Homes Company; and upon these was erected the first block of tenements. This is the neighborhood toward which the population has been setting with ever increasing congestion. Already in 1895 the Twenty-Second Ward contained nearly 200,000 souls. Between Forty-Ninth and Sixty-Second streets, west of Ninth Avenue, there are at least five blocks with more than 3000 tenants in each, and the conditions of the notorious Tenth Ward are certain to be reproduced here, if indeed they are not exceeded. In the Fifteenth Assembly District, some distance below, but on the same line, the first sociological canvass of the Federation of Churches had found the churches, schools, and other educational agencies marshaling a frontage of 756 feet on the street, while the saloon fronts stretched themselves over nearly a mile; so that, said the compiler of these pregnant facts, "saloon social ideals are minting themselves in the minds of the people at the ratio of seven saloon thoughts to one educational thought." It would not have been easy to find a spot better fitted for the experiment of restoring to the home its rights.

The Alfred Corning Clark Buildings, as they were called in recognition of the support of this public-spirited woman, have been occupied a year. When I went through them, the other day, I found all but five of the 373 apartments they contain occupied, and a very large waiting list of applicants for whom there was no room. The doctor alone, of all the tenants, had moved away, disappointed. He had settled on the estate, hoping to build up a practice among so many; but he could not make a living. The plan of the buildings, for which Ernest Flagg, a young and energetic architect, with a very practical interest in the welfare of the Other Half, has the credit, seems to me to realize the ideal of making homes under a common roof. The tenants appeared to take the same view of it. They were a notably contented lot. Their only objection was to the use of the common tubs in the basement laundry,--a sign that, to my mind, was rather favorable than otherwise, though it argued ill for the scheme of public wash houses on the Glasgow plan that has seemed so promising. They were selected tenants as to trustworthiness and desirability on that score, but they were all of the tenement house class. The rents are a little lower than for much poorer quarters in the surrounding tenements. The houses are built around central courts, with light and air in abundance, with fireproof stairs and steam-heated halls. There is not a dark passage anywhere. Within, there is entire privacy for the tenant; the partitions are deadened, so that sound is not transmitted from one apartment to another. Without, the houses have none of the discouraging barrack look. The architecture is distinctly pleasing. The few and simple rules laid down by the management have been readily complied with, as making for the benefit of all. A woman collects the rents, which are paid weekly in advance. The promise that the property will earn the five per cent. to which the company limits its dividends seems certain to be kept. There is nothing in sight to prevent it, everything to warrant the prediction.

The capital stock has since been increased to $2,000,000, and the erection has been begun of a new block of buildings in East Sixty-Fourth Street, within hail of Battle Row, of anciently warlike memory. James E. Ware & Son, the architects who, in the competition of 1879, won the prize for the improved tenements that marked the first departure from the boxlike barracks of old, drew the plans, embodying all the good features of the Clark Buildings with attractions of their own. A suburban colony is being developed by the company, in addition. It is not the least promising feature of its work that a very large proportion of its shareholders are workingmen, who have invested their savings in the enterprise, thus bearing witness to their faith and interest in it. Of the entire number of shareholders at the time of the first annual report, forty-five per cent, held less than ten shares each.

The success of these and previous efforts at the building of model tenements has had the desired effect of encouraging other attempts in the same direction. They represent the best that can be done in fighting the slum within the city. Homewood, the City and Suburban Homes Company's settlement in the country, stands for the way out that must eventually win the fight. That is the track that must be followed, and will be when we have found in rapid transit the key to the solution of our present perplexities. "In the country" hardly describes the site of the colony. It is within the Greater City, on Long Island, hardly an hour's journey by trolley from the City Hall, and only a short walk from the bay. Here the company has built a hundred cottages, and has room for two or three hundred more. Of the hundred houses, seventy-two had been sold when I was there last winter. They are handsome and substantial little houses, the lower story of brick, the upper of timber and stucco, each cottage standing in its own garden. The purchaser pays for the property in monthly payments extending over twenty years. A plan of life insurance, which protects the family and the company alike in the event of the death of the bread-winner, is included in the arrangement. The price of the cottages which so far have found owners has averaged about $3100, and the monthly installment, including the insurance premium, a trifle over $25. It follows that the poorest have not moved to Homewood. Its settlers include men with an income of $1200 or $1500 a year,--policemen, pilots, letter carriers, clerks, and teachers. This is as it should be. They represent the graduating class, as it were, from the city crowds. It is the province of the philanthropic tenement to prepare the next lot for moving up and out. Any attempt to hasten the process by taking a short cut could result only in failure and disappointment. The graduating class is large enough, however, to guarantee that it will not be exhausted by one Homewood. Before the houses were contracted for, without advertising or effort of any kind to make the thing known, more than eight hundred wage earners had asked to have their names put on the books as applicants for suburban homes.

Others had built model tenements and made them pay, but it was left to Mr. D. O. Mills to break ground in the field which Lord Rowton had filled with such signal success in London. The two Mills Houses, in Bleecker and Rivington streets, are as wide a departure as could well be imagined from the conventional type of lodging houses in New York. They are large and beautiful structures, which, for the price of a cot in one of the Bowery barracks, furnish their lodgers with as good a bed in a private room as the boarder in the Waldorf-Astoria enjoys. Indeed, it is said to be the very same in make and quality. There are baths without stint, smoking and writing rooms and games, and a free library; a laundry for those who can pay for having their washing done, and a separate one for such as prefer to do it themselves. There is a restaurant in the basement, in which a regular dinner of good quality is served at fifteen cents. The night's lodging is twenty cents. The dearest Bowery lodging houses charge twenty-five cents. The bedrooms are necessarily small, but they are clean and comfortable, well lighted and heated. The larger house, No. 1, in Bleecker Street, has room for 1554 guests; No. 2, in Rivington Street, for 600. Though this represents more than twelve per cent, of the capacity of all the cheap lodging houses in the city, both have been filled since they were opened, and crowds have often been turned away. The Bowery "hotels" have felt the competition. Their owners deny it, but the fact is apparent in efforts at improvements with which they were not justly chargeable before. Only the lowest, the ten-cent houses, are exempt from this statement. These attract a class of custom for which the Mills Houses do not compete. The latter are intended for the large number of decent mechanics, laborers, and men of small means, hunting for work, who are always afloat in a large city, and who neither seek nor wish charity. The plan and purpose of the builder cannot be better put than in his own words at the opening of the first house.

"No patron of the Mills Hotel," he said, "will receive more than he pays for, unless it be my hearty goodwill and good wishes. It is true that I have devoted thought, labor, and capital to a very earnest effort to help him, but only by enabling him to help himself. In doing the work on so large a scale, and in securing the utmost economies in purchases and in administration, I hope to give him a larger equivalent for his money than has hitherto been possible. He can, without scruple, permit me to offer him this advantage; but he will think better of himself, and will be a more self-reliant, manly man and a better citizen, if he knows that he is honestly paying for what he gets."

Mr. Mills's faith that the business of housing the homeless crowds in decency and comfort could be made to pay just as well as that of housing families in model tenements has been justified. Besides providing a fund sufficient for deterioration and replacement, the two houses have made a clear three per cent. profit on the investment of $1,500,000 which they represent. Beyond this, they have borne, and will bear increasingly, their own hand in settling with the saloon, which had no rival in the cheerlessness of the cheap lodging house or the boarding house back bedroom. Every philanthropic effort to fight it on that ground has drawn renewed courage and hope from Mr. Mills's work and success.

While I am writing, subscriptions are being made to the capital stock of a Woman's Hotel Company, that will endeavor to do for the self-supporting single women of our own city what Mr. Mills has done for the men. It is proposed to erect, at a cost of $800,000, a hotel capable of sheltering over 500 guests, at a price coming within reach of women earning wages as clerks, stenographers, nurses, etc. The number of women whose needs an establishment of the kind would meet is said to exceed 40,000. The Young Women's Christian Association alone receives every year requests enough for quarters to fill a score of such hotels, and can only refer the applicants to boarding houses. Experience in other cities shows that a woman's hotel or club can be managed and made profitable, and there seems to be little doubt that New York will be the next to furnish proof of it. It was the dream of A. T. Stewart, the merchant prince, to do this service for his city, just as he planned Garden City for a home colony for his clerks. It came out differently. The Long Island town became a cathedral city, and the home of wealth and fashion; his woman's hoarding house a great public hotel, far out of the reach of those he sought to benefit. It may be that the success of the banker's philanthropy will yet realize the dream of the merchant before the end of the century that saw his wealth, his great business, his very name, vanish as if they had never been, and even his bones denied, by ghoulish thieves, a rest in the grave. I like to think of it as a kind of justice to his memory, more eloquent than marble and brass in the empty crypt. Mills House No. 1 stands upon the site of Mr. Stewart's old home, where he dreamed his barren dream of benevolence to his kind.

Of all these movements the home is the keynote. That is the cheerful sign that shows light ahead. To the home it comes down in the end,--good government, bad government, and all the rest. As the homes of a community are, so is the community. New York has still the worst housing system in the world. Eight fifteenths of its people live in tenements, not counting the better class of flats, though legally they come under the definition. The blight of the twenty-five-foot lot remains, with the double-decker. But we can now destroy what is not fit to stand; we have done it, and our republic yet survives. The slum landlord would have had us believe that it must perish with his rookeries. We knew that to build decently improved a neighborhood, made the tenants better and happier, and reduced the mortality. Model tenement house building is now proving daily that such houses can be built safer and better every way for less money than the double-decker, by crossing the lot line. The dark hall is not a problem in the tenement built around a central court, for there is no common hall. The plan of the double-decker is shown to be wasteful of space and wall and capital. The model tenement pays, does not deteriorate, and keeps its tenants. After the lapse of ten years, I was the other day in Mr. A. T. White's Riverside Buildings in Brooklyn, which are still the best I know of, and found them, if anything, better houses than the day they were built. The stone steps of the stairways were worn: that was all the evidence of deterioration I saw. These, and Mr. White's other block of buildings on Hicks Street, which was built more than twenty years ago,-- occupied, all of them, by distinctly poor tenants,--have paid their owner over five per cent. right along. Practically, every such enterprise has the same story to tell. Dr. Gould found that only six per cent. of all the great model housing operations had failed to pay. All the rest were successful. That was the showing of Europe. It is the same here. Only the twenty-five-foot lot is in the way in New York.

It will continue to be in the way. A man who has one lot will build on it: it is his right. The state, which taxes his lot, has no right to confiscate it by forbidding him to make it yield him an income, on the plea that he might build something which would be a nuisance. But it can so order the building that it shall not be a nuisance: that is not only its right, but its duty. The best which can be made out of a twenty-five-foot lot is not good, but even that has not been made out of it yet. I have seen plans drawn by two young women architects in this city, the Misses Gannon and Hands, and approved by the Building Department, which let in an amount of light and air not dreamed of in the conventional type of double-decker, while providing detached stairs in a central court. It was not pretended that it was an ideal plan,--far from it; but it indicated clearly the track to be followed in dealing with the twenty-five-foot lot, seeing that we cannot get rid of it. The demand for light and air space must be sharpened and rigidly held to, and "discretion" to cut it down on any pretext must be denied, to the end of discouraging at least the building of double-deckers by the speculative landlord who has more than one lot, but prefers to build in the old way, in order that he may more quickly sell his houses, one by one.

With much evidence to the contrary in the big blocks of tenements that are going up on every hand, I think still we are tending in the right direction. I come oftener, nowadays, upon three tenements built on four lots, or two on three lots, than I used to. Indeed, there was a time when such a thing would have been considered wicked waste, or evidence of unsound mind in the builder. Houses are built now, as they were then, for profit. The business element must be there, or the business will fail. Philanthropy and five per cent. belong together in this field; but there is no more reason for allowing usurious interest to a man who makes a living by providing houses for the poor than for allowing it to a lender of money on security. In fact, there is less; for the former draws his profits from a source with which the welfare of the commonwealth is indissolubly bound up. The Tenement House Committee found that the double-deckers yield the landlord an average of ten per cent., attack the home, and are a peril to the community. Model tenements pay a safe five per cent., restore the home, and thereby strengthen the community. It comes down, then, as I said, to a simple question of the per cent. the builder will take. It should help his choice to know, as he cannot now help knowing, that the usurious profit is the price of good citizenship and human happiness, which suffer in the proportion in which the home is injured.

The problem of rent should be solved by the same formula, but not so readily. In the case of the builder the state can add force to persuasion, and so urge him along the path of righteousness. The only way to reach the rent collector would be for the municipality to enter the field as a competing landlord. Doubtless relief could be afforded that way. The Tenement House Committee found that the slum landlord charged the highest rents, sometimes as high as twenty-five per cent. He made no repairs. Model tenement house rents are lower, if anything, than those of the double-decker, with more space and better accommodations. Such a competition would have to be on a very large scale, however, to avail, and I am glad that New York has shown no disposition to undertake it yet. I would rather we, as a community, learned first a little more of the art of governing ourselves without scandal. Present relief from the burden that taxes the worker one fourth of his earnings for a roof over his head must be sought in the movement toward the suburbs that will follow the bridging of our rivers, and real rapid transit. On the island rents will always remain high, on account of the great land values. But I have often thought that if the city may not own new tenements, it might with advantage manage the old to the extent of licensing them to contain so many tenants on the basis of the air space, and no more. The suggestion was made when the tenement house question first came up for discussion, thirty years ago, but it was rejected then. The same thing is now proposed for rooms and workshops, as the means of getting the best of the sweating nuisance. Why not license the whole tenement, and with the money collected in the way of fees pay for the supervision of them by night and day? The squad of sanitary policemen now comprises for the Greater City some ninety men. Forty-one thousand tenements in the Borough of Manhattan alone, at three dollars each for the license, would pay the salaries of the entire body, and leave a margin. Seeing that their services are going exclusively to the tenements, it would not seem to be an unfair charge upon the landlords.

The home is the key to good citizenship. Unhappily for the great cities, there exists in them all a class that has lost the key or thrown it away. For this class, New York, until three years ago, had never made any provision. The police station lodging rooms, of which I have spoken, were not to be dignified by the term. These vile dens, in which the homeless of our great city were herded, without pretense of bed, of bath, of food, on rude planks, were the most pernicious parody on municipal charity, I verily believe, that any civilized community had ever devised. To escape physical and moral contagion in these crowds seemed humanly impossible. Of the innocently homeless lad they made a tramp by the shortest cut. To the old tramp they were indeed ideal provision, for they enabled him to spend for drink every cent he could beg or steal. With the stale beer dive, the free lunch counter, and the police lodging room at hand, his cup of happiness was full. There came an evil day, when the stale beer dive shut its doors and the free lunch disappeared for a season. The beer pump, which drained the kegs dry and robbed the stale beer collector of his ware, drove the dives out of business; the Raines law forbade the free lunch. Just at this time Theodore Roosevelt shut the police lodging rooms, and the tramp was literally left out in the cold, cursing reform and its fruits. It was the climax of a campaign a generation old, during which no one had ever been found to say a word in defense of these lodging rooms; yet nothing had availed to close them.

The city took lodgers on an old barge in the East River, that winter, and kept a register of them. We learned something from that. Of nearly 10,000 lodgers, one half were under thirty years old and in good health,--fat, in fact. The doctors reported them "well nourished." Among 100 whom I watched taking their compulsory bath, one night, only two were skinny; the others were stout, well-fed men, abundantly able to do a man's work. They all insisted that they were willing, too; but the moment inquiries began with a view of setting such to work as really wanted it, and sending the rest to the island as vagrants, their number fell off most remarkably. From between 400 and 500 who had crowded the barge and the pier sheds, the attendance fell on March 16, the day the investigation began, to 330, on the second day to 294, and on the third day to 171; by March 21 it had been cut down to 121. The problem of the honestly homeless, who were without means to pay for a bed even in a ten-cent lodging house, and who had a claim upon the city by virtue of residence in it, had dwindled to surprisingly small proportions. Of 9386 lodgers, 3622 were shown to have been here less than sixty days, and 968 less than a year. The old mistake, that there is always a given amount of absolutely homeless destitution in a city, and that it is to be measured by the number of those who apply for free lodging, had been reduced to a demonstration. The truth is that the opportunity furnished by the triple alliance of stale beer, free lunch, and free lodging at the police station was the open door to permanent and hopeless vagrancy.

A city lodging house was established, with decent beds, baths, and breakfast, and a system of investigation of the lodger's claim that is yet to be developed to useful proportions. The link that is missing is a farm school, for the training of young vagrants to habits of industry and steady work, as the alternative of the workhouse. Efforts to forge this link have failed so far, but in the good time that is coming, when we shall have learned the lesson that the unkindest thing that can be done to a young tramp is to let him go on tramping, and when magistrates shall blush to discharge him on the plea that "it is no crime to be poor in this country," they will succeed, and the tramp also we shall then have "druv into decency." When I look back now to the time, ten or fifteen years ago, when, night after night, with every police station filled, I found the old tenements in the "Bend" jammed with a reeking mass of human wrecks that huddled in hall and yard, and slept, crouching in shivering files, all the way up the stairs to the attic, it does seem as if we had come a good way, and as if all the turmoil and the bruises and the fighting had been worth while.

IV

THE TENANT

We have considered the problem of the tenement. Now about the tenant. How much of a problem is he? And how are we to go about solving his problem?

The government "slum inquiry," of which I have spoken before, gave us some facts about him. In New York it found 62.58 per cent. of the population of the slum to be foreign-born, whereas for the whole city the percentage of foreigners was only 43.23. While the proportion of illiteracy in all was only as 7.69 to 100, in the slum it was 46.65 per cent. That, with nearly twice as many saloons to a given number, there should be three times as many arrests in the slum as in the city at large need not be attributed to nationality, except indirectly in its possible responsibility for the saloons. I say "possible" advisedly. Anybody, I should think, whose misfortune it is to live in the slum might be expected to find in the saloon a refuge. I shall not quarrel with the other view of it. I am merely stating a personal impression. The fact that concerns us here is the great proportion of the foreign-born. Though the inquiry covered only a small section of a tenement district, the result may be accepted as typical.

We shall not, then, have to do with an American element in discussing this tenant, for even of the "natives" in the census, by far the largest share is made up of the children of the immigrant. Indeed, in New York only 4.77 per cent. of the slum population canvassed were shown to be of native parentage. The parents of 95.23 per cent. had come over the sea, to better themselves, it may be assumed. Let us see what they brought us, and what we have given them in return.

The Italians were in the majority where this census taker went. They were from the south of Italy, avowedly the worst of the Italian immigration which in the eight years from 1891 to 1898 gave us more than half a million of King Humbert's subjects. The exact number, as registered by the Emigration Bureau, was 502,592. In 1898, 58,613 came over, 36,086 of them with New York as their destination. The official year ends with June. In the six months from July 1 to December 31, the immigrants were sorted out upon a more intelligent plan than previously. The process as applied to the 30,470 Italians who were landed during that term yielded this result: from northern Italy, 4762; from southern Italy, 25,708. Of these latter a number came from Sicily, the island of the absentee landlord, where peasants die of hunger. I make no apology for quoting here the statement of an Italian officer, on duty in the island, to a staff correspondent of the "Tribuna" of Rome, a paper not to be suspected of disloyalty to United Italy. I take it from the "Evening Post:"--

"In the month of July I stopped on a march by a threshing floor where they were measuring grain. When the shares had been divided, the one who had cultivated the land received a single tumolo (less than a half bushel). The peasant, leaning on his spade, looked at his share as if stunned. His wife and their five children were standing by. From the painful toil of a year this was what was left to him with which to feed his family. The tears rolled silently down his cheeks."

These things occasionally help one to understand. Over against this picture there arises in my memory one from the Barge Office, where I had gone to see an Italian steamer come in. A family sat apart, ordered to wait by the inspecting officer; in the group an old man, worn and wrinkled, who viewed the turmoil with the calmness of one having no share in it. The younger members formed a sort of bulwark around him.

"Your father is too old," said the official.

Two young women and a boy of sixteen rose to their feet at once. "Are not we young enough to work for him?" they said. The boy showed his strong arms.

It is charged against this Italian immigrant that he is dirty, and the charge is true. He lives in the darkest of slums, and pays rent that ought to hire a decent flat. To wash, water is needed; and we have a law which orders tenement landlords to put it on every floor, so that their tenants may have the chance. And it is not yet half a dozen years since one of the biggest tenement house landlords in the city, the wealthiest church corporation in the land, attacked the constitutionality of this statute rather than pay a couple of hundred dollars for putting water into two old buildings, as the Board of Health had ordered, and came near upsetting the whole structure of tenement house law upon which our safety depends. He is ignorant, it is said, and that charge is also true. I doubt if one of the family in the Barge Office could read or write his own name. Yet would you fear especial danger to our institutions, to our citizenship, from these four? He lives cheaply, crowds, and underbids even the Jew in the sweatshop. I can myself testify to the truth of these statements. Only this spring I was the umpire in a quarrel between the Jewish tailors and the factory inspector whom they arraigned before the Governor on charges of inefficiency. The burden of their grievance was that the Italians were underbidding them in their own market, which of course the factory inspector could not prevent. Yet, even so, the evidence is not that the Italian always gets the best of it. I came across a family once working on "knee-pants." "Twelve pants, ten cents," said the tailor, when there was work. "Ve work for dem sheenies," he explained. "Ven dey has work, ve gets some; ven dey hasn't, ve don't." He was an unusually gifted tailor as to English, but apparently not as to business capacity. In the Astor tenements, in Elizabeth Street, where we found forty-three families living in rooms intended for sixteen, I saw women finishing "pants" at thirty cents a day. Some of the garments were of good grade, and some of poor; some of them were soldiers' trousers, made for the government; but whether they received five, seven, eight, or ten cents a pair, it came to thirty cents a day, except in a single instance, in which two women, sewing from five in the morning till eleven at night, were able, being practiced hands, to finish forty-five "pants" at three and a half cents a pair, and so made together over a dollar and a half.

They were content, even happy. I suppose it seemed wealth to them, coming from a land where a Parisian investigator of repute found three lire (not quite sixty cents) per month a girl's wages.

I remember one of those flats, poor and dingy, yet with signs of the instinctive groping toward orderly arrangement which I have observed so many times, and take to be evidence that in better surroundings much might be made of these people. Clothes were hung to dry on a line strung the whole length of the room. Upon couches by the wall some men were snoring. They were the boarders. The "man" was out shoveling snow with the midnight shift. By a lamp with brown paper shade, over at the window, sat two women sewing. One had a baby on her lap. Two sweet little cherubs, nearly naked, slept on a pile of unfinished "pants," and smiled in their sleep. A girl of six or seven dozed in a child's rocker between the two workers, with her head hanging down on one side; the mother propped it up with her elbow as she sewed. They were all there, and happy in being together even in such a place. On a corner shelf burned a night lamp before a print of the Mother of God, flanked by two green bottles, which, seen at a certain angle, made quite a festive show.

Complaint is made that the Italian promotes child labor. His children work at home on "pants" and flowers at an hour when they ought to have been long in bed. Their sore eyes betray the little flower-makers when they come tardily to school. Doubtless there are such cases, and quite too many of them; yet, in the very block which I have spoken of, the investigation conducted for the Tenement House Committee by the University Department of Sociology of Columbia College, under Professor Franklin H. Giddings, discovered of 196 children of school age only 23 at work or at home, and in the next block only 27 out of 215. That was the showing of the foreign population all the way through. Of 225 Russian Jewish children only 15 were missing from school, and of 354 little Bohemians only 21. The overcrowding of the schools and their long waiting lists occasionally furnished the explanation why they were not there. Professor Giddings reported, after considering all the evidence: "The foreign-born population of the city is not, to any great extent, forcing children of legal school age into money-earning occupations. On the contrary, this population shows a strong desire to have its children acquire the common rudiments of education. If the city does not provide liberally and wisely for the satisfaction of this desire, the blame for the civic and moral dangers that will threaten our community, because of ignorance, vice, and poverty, must rest on the whole public, not on our foreign-born residents." It is satisfactory to know that the warning has been heeded, and that soon there will be schools enough to hold all the children who come. Now, since September 1, 1899, the new factory law reaches also the Italian flowermaker in his home, and that source of waste will be stopped.

He is clannish, this Italian; he gambles and uses a knife, though rarely on anybody not of his own people; he "takes what he can get," wherever anything is free, as who would not, coming to the feast like a starved wolf? There was nothing free where he came from. Even the salt was taxed past a poor man's getting any of it. Lastly, he buys fraudulent naturalization papers, and uses them. I shall plead guilty for him to every one of these counts. They are all proven. Gambling is his besetting sin. He is sober, industrious, frugal, enduring beyond belief, but he will gamble on Sunday and quarrel over his cards, and when he sticks his partner in the heat of the quarrel, the partner is not apt to tell. He prefers to bide his time. Yet there has lately been evidence once or twice in the surrender of an assassin by his countrymen that the old vendetta is being shelved, and a new idea of law and justice is breaking through. As to the last charge: our Italian is not dull. With his intense admiration for the land where a dollar a day waits upon the man with a shovel, he can see no reason why he should not accept the whole "American plan" with ready enthusiasm. It is a good plan. To him it sums itself up in the statement: a dollar a day for the shovel; two dollars for the shovel with a citizen behind it. And he takes the papers and the two dollars.

He came here for a chance to live. Of politics, social ethics, he knows nothing. Government in his old home existed only for his oppression. Why should he not attach himself with his whole loyal soul to the plan of government in his new home that offers to boost him into the place of his wildest ambition, a "job on the streets,"--that is, in the Street-Cleaning Department,--and asks no other return than that he shall vote as directed? Vote! Not only he, but his cousins and brothers and uncles will vote as they are told, to get Pietro the job he covets. If it pleases the other man, what is it to him for whom he votes? He is after the job. Here, ready-made to the hand of the politician, is such material as he never saw before. For Pietro's loyalty is great. As a police detective, one of his own people, once put it to me: "He got a kind of an idea, or an old rule: an eye for an eye; do to another as you'd be done by; if he don't squeal on you, you stick by him, no matter what the consequences." This "kind of an idea" is all he has to draw upon for an answer to the question if the thing is right. But the question does not arise. Why should it? Was he not told by the agitators whom the police jailed at home that in a republic all men are made happy by means of the vote? And is there not proof of it? It has made him happy, has it not? And the man who bought his vote seems to like it. Well, then?

Very early Pietro discovered that it was every man for himself, in the chase of the happiness which this powerful vote had in keeping. He was robbed by the padrone--that is, the boss--when he came over, fleeced on his steamship fare, made to pay for getting a job, and charged three prices for board and lodging and extras while working in the railroad gang. The boss had a monopoly, and Pietro was told that it was maintained by his "divvying" with some railroad official. Rumor said, a very high-up official, and that the railroad was in politics in the city; that is to say, dealt in votes. When the job gave out, the boss packed him into the tenement he had bought with his profits on the contract; and if Pietro had a family, told him to take in lodgers and crowd his flat, as the Elizabeth Street tenements were crowded, so as to make out the rent, and to never mind the law. The padrone was a politician, and had a pull. He was bigger than the law, and it was the votes he traded in that did it all. Now it was Pietro's turn. With his vote he could buy what to him seemed wealth. In the muddle of ideas, that was the one which stood out. When citizen papers were offered him for $12.50, he bought them quickly, and got his job on the street.

It was the custom of the country. If there was any doubt about it, the proof was furnished when Pietro was arrested through the envy and plotting of the opposition boss last fall. Distinguished counsel, employed by the machine, pleaded his case in court. Pietro felt himself to be quite a personage, and he was told that he was safe from harm, though a good deal of dust might be kicked up; because, when it came down to that, both the bosses were doing the same kind of business. I quote from the report of the State Superintendent of Elections of January, 1899: "In nearly every case of illegal registration, the defendant was represented by eminent counsel who were identified with the Democratic organization, among them being three assistants to the Corporation counsel. My deputies arrested Rosario Calecione and Giuseppe Marrone, both of whom appeared to vote at the fifth election district of the Sixth Assembly District; Marrone being the Democratic captain of the district, and, it was charged, himself engaged in the business of securing fraudulent naturalization papers. In both of these cases Farriello had procured the naturalization papers for the men for a consideration. They were subsequently indicted. Marrone and Calecione were bailed by the Democratic leader of the Sixth Assembly District."

The business, says the State Superintendent, is carried on "to an enormous extent." It appears, then, that Pietro has already "got on to" the American plan as the slum presented it to him, and has in good earnest become a problem. I guessed as much from the statement of a Tammany politician to me, a year ago, that every Italian voter in his district got his "old two" on election day. He ought to know, for he held the purse. Suppose, now, we speak our minds as frankly, for once, and put the blame where it belongs. Will it be on Pietro? And upon this showing, who ought to be excluded, when it comes to that?

The slum census taker did not cross the Bowery. Had he done so, he would have come upon the refugee Jew, the other economic marplot of whom complaint is made with reason. If his Nemesis has overtaken him in the Italian, certainly he challenged that fate. He did cut wages by his coming. He was starving, and he came in shoals. In fourteen years more than 400,000 Jewish immigrants have landed in New York.[3] They had to have work and food, and they got both as they could. In the strife they developed qualities that were anything but pleasing. They herded like cattle. They had been so herded by Christian rulers, a despised and persecuted race, through the centuries. Their very coming was to escape from their last inhuman captivity in a Christian state. They lied, they were greedy, they were charged with bad faith. They brought nothing,--neither money nor artisan skill,--nothing but their consuming energy, to our land, and their one gift was their greatest offense. One might have pointed out that they had been trained to lie, for their safety; had been forbidden to work at trades, to own land; had been taught for a thousand years, with the scourge and the stake, that only gold could buy them freedom from torture. But what was the use? The charges were true. The Jew was--he still is--a problem of our slum.

[Footnote 3: According to the register of the United Hebrew Charities, between October 1, 1884, and March 1, 1899, the number was 402,181.]

And yet, if ever there was material for citizenship, this Jew is such material. Alone of all our immigrants he comes to us without a past. He has no country to renounce, no ties to forget. Within him there burns a passionate longing for a home to call his, a country which will own him, that waits only for the spark of such another love to spring into flame which nothing can quench. Waiting for it, all his energies are turned into his business. He is not always choice in method; he often offends. But he succeeds. He is the yeast of any slum, if given time. If it will not let him go, it must rise with him. The charity managers in London said it, when we looked through their slums some years ago: "The Jews have renovated Whitechapel." I, for one, am a firm believer in this Jew, and in his boy. Ignorant they are, but with a thirst for knowledge that surmounts any barrier. The boy takes all the prizes in the school. His comrades sneer that he will not fight. Neither will he when there is nothing to be gained by it. But I believe that, should the time come when the country needs fighting men, the son of the despised immigrant Jew will resurrect on American soil, the first that bade him welcome, the old Maccabee type, and set an example for all the rest of us to follow.

For fifteen years he has been in the public eye as the vehicle and promoter of sweating, and much severe condemnation has been visited upon him with good cause. He had to do something, and he took to the clothes-maker's trade as that which was most quickly learned. The increasing crowds, the tenement, and his grinding poverty made the soil, wherein the evil thing grew rank. Yet the real sweater is the manufacturer, not the workman. It is just a question of expense to the manufacturer. By letting out his work on contract, he can save the expense of running his factory and delay longer making his choice of styles. The Jew is the victim of the mischief quite as much as he has helped it on. Back of the manufacturer there is still another sweater,--the public. Only by its sufferance of the bargain counter and of sweatshop-made goods has the nuisance existed as long as it has. I am glad to believe that its time is passing away. The law has driven the sweatshops out of the tenements, and so deprived them of one of their chief props: there was no rent at all to pay there. Child labor, which only four years ago the Reinhard Committee characterized as "one of the most extensive evils now existing in the city of New York, a constant and grave menace to the welfare of its people," has been practically banished from the tailoring trade. What organization among the workers had failed to effect is apparently going to be accomplished by direct pressure of an outraged public opinion. Already manufacturers are returning to their own factories, and making capital of the fact among their customers. The new law, which greatly extends the factory inspector's power over sweatshops, is an expression of this enlightened sentiment. It will put New York a long stride ahead, and quite up to Massachusetts. The inspector's tag has proved, where the law was violated, an effective weapon. It suspends all operation of the shop and removal of the goods until the orders of the inspector have been obeyed. But the tag which shall finally put an end to sweating, and restore decent conditions, is not the factory inspector's, I am persuaded, but a trades union label, which shall deserve public confidence and receive it. We have much to learn yet, all of us. I think I can see the end of this trouble, however, when the Italian's triumph in the sweatshop shall have proved but a barren victory, to his own gain.

In all I have said so far, in these papers, I have not gone beyond the limits of the old city,--of Manhattan Island, in fact. I want now to glance for a moment at the several attempts made at colonizing refugee Jews in this part of the country. Brownsville was one of the earliest. Its projector was a manufacturer, and its motive profit. The result was the familiar one,--as nasty a little slum as ever the East Side had to show. We have it on our hands now in the Greater City,--it came in with Brooklyn,--and it is not a gain. Down in southern New Jersey several colonies were started, likewise by speculators, in the persecution of the early eighties, and these also failed. The soil was sandy and poor, and, thrown upon their own resources in a strange and unfriendly neighborhood, with unfamiliar and unremunerative toil, the colonists grew discouraged and gave up in despair. The colonies were approaching final collapse, when the managers of the Baron de Hirsch Fund in New York, who had started and maintained a successful colony at Woodbine, in the same neighborhood, took them under the arms and inaugurated a new plan. They persuaded several large clothing contractors in this city to move their plants down to the villages, where they would be assured of steady hands, not so easily affected by strikes. For strikes in sweatshops are often enough the alternative of starvation. Upon the land there would be no starvation. The managers of the Fund built factories, bought the old mortgages on the farms, and put up houses for the families which the contractors brought down with them. This effort at transplanting the crowd from the Ghetto to the soil has now been going on for a year. At latest account, eight contractors and two hundred and fifty families had been moved out. The colonies had taken on a new lease of life and apparent prosperity. While it is yet too early to pass sober judgment, there seems to be good ground for hoping that a real way out has been found that shall restore the Jew, at least in a measure, to the soil from which he was barred so long. The experiment is of exceeding interest. The hopes of its projectors that a purely farming community might be established have not been realized. Perhaps it was too much to expect. By bringing to the farmers their missing market, and work to the surplus population, the mixed settlement plan bids fair to prove a step in the desired direction.

Some 18,500 acres are now held by Jewish colonists in New Jersey. In the New England States, in the last eight years, 600 abandoned farms have been occupied and are cultivated by refugees from Russia. As a dairy farmer and a poultry raiser, the Jew has more of an immediate commercial grip on the situation and works with more courage. At Woodbine, sixty-five boys and girls are being trained in an agricultural school that has won the whole settlement the friendly regard of the neighborhood. Of its pupils, eleven came out of tailor shops, and ten had been office boys, messengers, or newsboys. To these, and to the trade schools now successfully operated by the de Hirsch Fund, we are to look in the next generation for the answer to the old taunt that the Jew is a trader, and not fit to be either farmer or craftsman, and for the solution of the problem which he now presents in the slum.

I have spoken at length of the Jew and the Italian, because they are our present problem. Yesterday it was the Irishman and the Bohemian. To-morrow it may be the Greek, who already undersells the Italian from his pushcart in the Fourth Ward, and the Syrian, who can give Greek, Italian, and Jew points at a trade. From Dalmatia a new immigration has begun to come, and there are signs of its working further east in the Balkan states, where there is no telling what is in store for us. How to absorb them all safely is the question. Doubtless the Irishman, having absorbed us politically, would be glad to free us from all concern on that score by doing a like favor for them. But we should not get the best of the slum that way; it would get the best of us, instead. Would I shut out the newcomers? Sometimes, looking at it from the point of view of the Barge Office and the sweatshop, I think I would. Then there comes up the recollection of a picture of the city of Prague that hangs in a Bohemian friend's parlor, here in New York. I stood looking at it one day, and noticed in the foreground cannon that pointed in over the city. I spoke of it, unthinking, and said to my host that they should be trained, if against an enemy, the other way. The man's eye flashed fire. "Ha!" he cried, "here, yes!" When I think of that, I do not want to shut the door.

Again, there occurs to me an experience the police had last summer in Mulberry Street. They were looking for a murderer, and came upon a nest of Italian thugs who lived by blackmailing their countrymen. They were curious about them, and sent their names to Naples with a request for information. There came back such a record as none of the detectives had ever seen or heard of before. All of them were notorious criminals, who had been charged with every conceivable crime, from burglary to kidnapping and "maiming," and some not to be conceived of by the American mind. Five of them together had been sixty-three times in jail, and one no less than twenty-one times. Yet, though they were all "under special surveillance," they had come here without let or hindrance within a year. When I recall that, I want to shut the door quick. I sent the exhibit to Washington at the time. But then, again, when I think of Mrs. Michelangelo in her poor mourning for one child run over and killed, wiping her tears away and going bravely to work to keep the home together for the other five until the oldest shall be old enough to take her father's place; and when, as now, there strays into my hand the letter from my good friend, the "woman doctor" in the slum, when her father had died, in which she wrote: "The little scamps of the street have been positively pathetic; they have made such shy, boyish attempts at friendliness. One little chap offered to let me hold his top while it was spinning, in token of affection,"--when I read that, I have not the heart to shut anybody out.

Except, of course, the unfit, the criminal and the pauper, cast off by their own, and the man brought over here merely to put money into the pockets of the steamship agent, the padrone, and the mine owner. We have laws to bar these out. Suppose we begin by being honest with ourselves and the immigrant, and enforcing our own laws. In spite of a healthy effort at the port of New York,--I can only speak for that,--under the present administration, that has not yet been done. When the door has been shut and locked against the man who left his country for his country's good, whether by its "assistance" or not, and when trafficking in the immigrant for private profit has been stopped, then, perhaps, we shall be better able to decide what degree of ignorance in him constitutes unfitness for citizenship and cause for shutting him out. Perchance then, also, we shall hear less of the cant about his being a peril to the republic. Doubtless ignorance is a peril, but the selfishness that trades upon ignorance is a much greater. He came to us without a country, ready to adopt such a standard of patriotism as he found, at its face value, and we gave him the rear tenement and slum politics. If he accepted the standard, whose fault was it? His being in such a hurry to vote that he could not wait till the law made him a citizen was no worse, to my mind, than the treachery of the "upper class" native, who refuses to go to the polls for fear he may rub up against him there. This last let us settle with first, and see what remains of our problem. We can approach it honestly, then, at all events.

When the country was in the throes of the silver campaign, the newspapers told the story of an old laborer who went to the sub-treasury and demanded to see the "boss." He undid the strings of an old leathern purse with fumbling fingers, and counted out more than two hundred dollars in gold eagles, the hoard of a lifetime of toil and self-denial. They were for the government, he said. He had not the head to understand all the talk that was going, but he gathered from what he heard that the government was in trouble, and that somehow it was about not having gold enough. So he had brought what he had. He owed it all to the country, and now that she needed it he had come to give it back. The man was an Irishman. Very likely he was enrolled in Tammany and voted her ticket. I remember a tenement at the bottom of a back alley over on the East Side, where I once went visiting with the pastor of a mission chapel. Up in the attic there was a family of father and daughter in two rooms that had been made out of one by dividing off the deep dormer window. It was midwinter, and they had no fire. He was a peddler, but the snow had stalled his pushcart and robbed them of their only other source of income, a lodger who hired cot room in the attic for a few cents a night. The daughter was not able to work. But she said, cheerfully, that they were "getting along." When it came out that she had not tasted solid food for many days, was starving, in fact,--indeed, she died within a year, of the slow starvation of the tenements that parades in the mortality returns under a variety of scientific names which all mean the same thing,--she met her pastor's gentle chiding with the excuse, "Oh, your church has many poorer than I. I don't want to take your money."

These were Germans, ordinarily held to be close-fisted; but I found that in their dire distress they had taken in a poor old man who was past working, and had kept him all winter, sharing with him what they had. He was none of theirs; they hardly even knew him, as it appeared. It was enough that he was "poorer than they," and lonely and hungry and cold.

It was over here that the children of Dr. Elsing's Sunday school gave out of the depth of their poverty fifty-four dollars in pennies to be hung on the Christmas tree as their offering to the persecuted Armenians. One of their teachers told me of a Bohemian family that let the holiday dinner she brought them stand and wait, while they sent out to bid to the feast four little ragamuffins of the neighborhood who else would have gone hungry. I remember well a teacher in one of the Children's Aid Society's schools, herself a tenement child, who, with breaking heart, but brave face, played and sang the children's Christmas carols with them rather than spoil their pleasure, while her only sister lay dying at home.

I might keep on and fill many pages with instances of that kind, which simply go to prove that our poor human nature is at least as robust on Avenue A as up on Fifth Avenue, if it has half a chance, and often enough to restore one's faith in it, with no chance at all; and I might set over against it the product of sordid and mean environment which one has never far to seek. Good and evil go together in the tenements as in the fine houses, and the evil sticks out sometimes merely because it lies nearer the surface. The point is that the good does outweigh the bad, and that the virtues that turn the balance are after all those that make for good citizenship anywhere, while the faults are oftenest the accidents of ignorance and lack of training, which it is the business of society to correct. I recall my discouragement when I looked over the examination papers of a batch of candidates for police appointment,-- young men largely the product of our public schools in this city and elsewhere,--and read in them that five of the original New England States were "England, Ireland, Scotland, Belfast, and Cork;" that the Fire Department ruled New York in the absence of the Mayor,--I have sometimes wished it did, and that he would stay away awhile; and that Lincoln was murdered by Ballington Booth. But we shall agree, no doubt, that the indictment of these papers was not of the men who wrote them, but of the school that stuffed its pupils with useless trash, and did not teach them to think. Neither have I forgotten that it was one of these very men who, having failed, and afterward got a job as a bridge policeman, on his first pay day went straight from his post, half frozen as he was, to the settlement worker who had befriended him and his sick father, and gave him five dollars for "some one who was poorer than they." Poorer than they! What worker among the poor has not heard it? It is the charity of the tenement that covers a multitude of sins. There were thirteen in this policeman's family, and his wages were the biggest item of income in the house.

Jealousy, envy, and meanness wear no fine clothes and masquerade under no smooth speeches in the slums. Often enough it is the very nakedness of the virtues that makes us stumble in our judgment. I have in mind the "difficult case" that confronted some philanthropic friends of mine in a rear tenement on Twelfth Street, in the person of an aged widow, quite seventy I should think, who worked uncomplainingly for a sweater all day and far into the night, pinching and saving and stinting herself, with black bread and chicory coffee as her only fare, in order that she might carry her pitiful earnings to her big, lazy lout of a son in Brooklyn. He never worked. My friends' difficulty was a very real one, for absolutely every attempt to relieve the widow was wrecked upon her mother heart. It all went over the river. Yet one would not have had her different.

Sometimes it is only the unfamiliar setting that shocks. When an East Side midnight burglar, discovered and pursued, killed a tenant who blocked his way of escape, a few weeks ago, his "girl" gave him up to the police. But it was not because he had taken human life. "He was good to me," she explained to the captain whom she told where to find him, "but since he robbed the church I had no use for him." He had stolen, it seems, the communion service in a Staten Island church. The thoughtless laughed. But in her ignorant way she was only trying to apply the standards of morality as they had been taught her. Stunted, bemuddled, as they were, I think I should prefer to take my chances with her rather than with the woman of wealth and luxury who, some years ago, gave a Christmas party to her lap-dog, as on the whole the sounder of the two, and by far the more hopeful.

All of which is merely saying that the country is all right, and the people are to be trusted with the old faith in spite of the slum. And it is true, if we remember to put it that way,--in spite of the slum. There is nothing in the slum to warrant that faith save human nature as yet uncorrupted. How long it is to remain so is altogether a question of the sacrifices we are willing to make in our fight with the slum. As yet, we are told by the officials having to do with the enforcement of the health ordinances, which come closer to the life of the individual than any other kind, that the poor in the tenements are "more amenable to the law than the better class." It is of the first importance, then, that we should have laws deserving of their respect, and that these laws should be enforced, lest they conclude that the whole thing is a sham. Respect for law is a very powerful bar against the slum. But what, for instance, must the poor Jew understand, who is permitted to buy a live hen at the market, yet neither to kill nor keep it in his tenement, and who on his feast day finds a whole squad of policemen detailed to follow him around and see that he does not do any of the things with his fowl for which he must have bought it? Or the day laborer, who drinks his beer in a "Raines law hotel," where brick sandwiches, consisting of two pieces of bread with a brick between, are set out on the counter, in derision of the state law which forbids the serving of drinks without "meals"? (The Stanton Street saloon keeper who did that was solemnly acquitted by a jury.) Or the boy, who may buy fireworks on the Fourth of July, but not set them off? These are only ridiculous instances of an abuse that pervades our community life to an extent that constitutes one of the gravest perils. Insincerity of that kind is not lost on our fellow citizen by adoption, who is only anxious to fall in with the ways of the country; and especially is it not lost on his boy.

We shall see how it affects him. He is the one for whom we are waging the battle with the slum. He is the to-morrow that sits to-day drinking in the lesson of the prosperity of the big boss who declared with pride upon the witness stand that he rules New York, that judges pay him tribute, and that only when he says so a thing "goes;" and that it is all for what he can get out of it, "just the same as everybody else." He sees corporations to-day pay blackmail and rob the people in return, quite according to the schedule of Hester Street. Only there it is the police who charge the peddler twenty cents, while here it is the politicians taking toll of the franchises, twenty per cent. Wall Street is not ordinarily reckoned in the slum, because of certain physical advantages; but, upon the evidence of the day, I think we shall have to conclude that the advantage ends there. The boy who is learning such lessons,--how is it with him?

The president of the Society for the Prevention of Cruelty to Children says that children's crime is increasing, and he ought to know. The managers of the Children's Aid Society, after forty-six years of wrestling with the slum for the boy, in which they have lately seemed to get the upper hand, say in this year's report that on the East Side children are growing up in certain districts "entirely neglected," and that the number of such children "increases beyond the power of philanthropic and religious bodies to cope properly with their needs." In the Tompkins Square Lodging House the evening classes are thinning out, and the keeper wails: "Those with whom we have dealt of late have not been inclined to accept this privilege; how to make night school attractive to shiftless, indifferent street boys is a difficult problem to solve."

Perhaps it is only that he has lost the key. Across the square, the Boys' Club of St. Mark's Place, that began with a handful, counts five thousand members to-day, and is seeking a place to build a house of its own. The school census man announces that no boy in that old stronghold of the "bread or blood" brigade need henceforth loiter in the street because there is not room in the public school, and the brigade has disbanded for want of recruits. The shop is being shut against the boy, and the bars let down at the playground. But from Tompkins Square, nevertheless, came Jacob Beresheim, whose story I shall tell you presently.

V

THE GENESIS OF THE GANG

Jacob Beresheim was fifteen when he was charged with murder. It is now more than three years ago, but the touch of his hand is cold upon mine, with mortal fear, as I write. Every few minutes, during our long talk on the night of his arrest and confession, he would spring to his feet, and, clutching my arm as a drowning man catches at a rope, demand with shaking voice, "Will they give me the chair?" The assurance that boys were not executed quieted him only for the moment. Then the dread and the horror were upon him again.

Of his crime the less said the better. It was the climax of a career of depravity that differed from other such chiefly in the opportunities afforded by an environment which led up to and helped shape it. My business is with that environment. The man is dead, the boy in jail. But unless I am to be my brother's jail keeper, merely, the iron bars do not square the account of Jacob with society. Society exists for the purpose of securing justice to its members, appearances to the contrary notwithstanding. When it fails in this, the item is carried on the ledger with interest and compound interest toward a day of reckoning that comes surely with the paymaster. We have heard the chink of his coin on the counter, these days, in the unblushing revelations before the Mazet Committee of degraded citizenship, of the murder of the civic conscience, and in the applause that hailed them. And we have begun to understand that these are the interest on Jacob's account, older, much older than himself. He is just an item carried on the ledger. But with that knowledge the account is at last in a way of getting squared. Let us see how it stands.

We shall take Jacob as a type of the street boy on the East Side, where he belonged. What does not apply to him in the review applies to his class. But there was very little of it indeed that he missed or that missed him.

He was born in a tenement in that section where the Tenement House Committee found 324,000 persons living out of sight and reach of a green spot of any kind, and where sometimes the buildings, front, middle, and rear, took up ninety-three per cent. of all the space on the block. Such a home as he had was there, and of the things that belonged to it he was the heir. The sunlight was not among them. It "never entered" there. Darkness and discouragement did, and dirt. Later on, when he took to the dirt as his natural weapon in his battles with society, it was said of him that it was the only friend that stuck to him, and it was true. Very early the tenement gave him up to the street. The thing he took with him as the one legacy of home was the instinct for the crowd, which meant that the tenement had wrought its worst mischief upon him: it had smothered that in him around which character is built. The more readily did he fall in with the street and its ways. Character implies depth, a soil, and growth. The street is all surface: nothing grows there; it hides only a sewer.

It taught him gambling as its first lesson, and stealing as the next. The two are never far apart. From shooting craps behind the "cop's" back to filching from the grocer's stock or plundering a defenseless peddler is only a step. There is in both the spice of law-breaking that appeals to the shallow ambition of the street as heroic. Occasionally the raids have a comic tinge. A German grocer wandered into police headquarters the other day, with an appeal for protection against the boys.

"Vat means dot 'cheese it'?" he asked, rubbing his bald head in helpless bewilderment. "Efery dime dey says 'cheese it,' somedings vas gone."

To the lawlessness of the street the home opposes no obstacle, as we have seen. Until very recently the school did not. It might have more to offer even now. There are, at least, schools where there were none then, and so much is gained; also, they are getting better, but too many of them, in my unprofessional judgment, need yet to be made over, until they are fit to turn out whole, sound boys, instead of queer manikins stuffed with information for which they have no use, and which is none of their business anyhow. It seemed to me sometimes, when watching the process of cramming the school course with the sum of human knowledge and conceit, as if it all meant that we distrusted nature's way of growing a man from a boy, and had set out to show her a shorter cut. A common result was the kind of mental befogment that had Abraham Lincoln murdered by Ballington Booth, and a superficiality, a hopeless slurring of tasks, that hitched perfectly with the spirit of the street, and left nothing to be explained in the verdict of the reformatory, "No moral sense." There was no moral sense to be got out of the thing, for there was little sense of any kind in it. The boy was not given a chance to be honest with himself by thinking a thing through; he came naturally to accept as his mental horizon the headlines in his penny paper and the literature of the Dare-Devil-Dan-the-Death-Dealing-Monster-of-Dakota order, which comprise the ordinary 鍕 thetic equipment of the slum. The mystery of his further development into the tough need not perplex anybody.

But Jacob Beresheim had not even the benefit of such schooling as there was to be had. He did not go to school, and nobody cared. There was indeed a law directing that every child should go, and a corps of truant officers to catch him if he did not; but the law had been a dead letter for a quarter of a century. There was no census to tell what children ought to be in school, and no place but a jail to put those in who shirked. Jacob was allowed to drift. From the time he was twelve till he was fifteen, he told me, he might have gone to school three weeks,--no more.

Church and Sunday school missed him. I was going to say that they passed by on the other side, remembering the migration of the churches uptown, as the wealthy moved out of, and the poor into, the region south of Fourteenth Street. But that would hardly be fair. They moved after their congregations;

but they left nothing behind. In the twenty years that followed the war, while enough to people a large city moved in downtown, the number of churches there was reduced from 141 to 127. Fourteen Protestant churches moved out. Only two Roman Catholic churches and a synagogue moved in. I am not aware that there has been any large increase of churches in the district since, but we have seen that the crowding has not slackened pace. Jacob had no trouble in escaping the Sunday school as he had escaped the public school. His tribe will have none until the responsibility incurred in the severance of church and state sits less lightly on a Christian community, and the church, from a mob, shall have become an army, with von Moltke's plan of campaign, "March apart, fight together." The Christian church is not alone in its failure. The Jew's boy is breaking away from safe moorings rather faster than his brother of the new dispensation. The church looks on, but it has no cause for congratulation. He is getting nothing in place of that which he lost, and the result is bad. There is no occasion for profound theories about it. The facts are plain enough. The new freedom has something to do with it, but neglect to look after the young has quite as much. Apart from its religious aspect, seen from the angle of the community's interest wholly, the matter is of the gravest import.

What the boy's play has to do with building character in him Froebel has told us. Through it, he showed us, the child "first perceives moral relations," and he made that the basis of the kindergarten and all common-sense education. That prop was knocked out. New York never had a children's playground till within the last year. Truly it seemed, as Abram S. Hewitt said, as if in the early plan of our city the children had not been thought of at all. Such moral relations as Jacob was able to make out ran parallel with the gutter always, and counter to law and order as represented by the policeman and the landlord. The landlord had his windows to mind, and the policeman his lamps and the city ordinances which prohibit even kite-flying below Fourteenth Street where the crowds are. The ball had no chance at all. It is not two years since a boy was shot down by a policeman for the heinous offense of playing football in the street on Thanksgiving Day. But a boy who cannot kick a ball around has no chance of growing up a decent and orderly citizen. He must have his childhood, so that he may be fitted to give to the community his manhood. The average boy is just like a little steam engine with steam always up. The play is his safety valve. With the landlord in the yard and the policeman on the street sitting on his safety valve and holding it down, he is bound to explode. When he does, when he throws mud and stones and shows us the side of him which the gutter developed, we are shocked and marvel much what our boys are coming to, as if we had any right to expect better treatment of them. I doubt if Jacob, in the whole course of his wizened little life, had ever a hand in an honest game that was not haunted by the dread of the avenging policeman. That he was not "doing anything" was no defense. The mere claim was proof that he was up to mischief of some sort. Besides, the policeman was usually right. Play in such a setting becomes a direct incentive to mischief in a healthy boy. Jacob was a healthy enough little animal.

Such fun as he had he got out of law-breaking in a small way. In this he was merely following the ruling fashion. Laws were apparently made for no other purpose that he could see. Such a view as he enjoyed of their makers and executors at election seasons inspired him with seasonable enthusiasm, but hardly with awe. A slogan, now, like that raised by Tammany's late candidate for district attorney,--"To hell with reform!"--was something he could grasp. Of what reform meant he had only the vaguest notion, but the thing had the right ring to it. Roosevelt preaching enforcement of law was from the first a "lobster" to him, not to be taken seriously. It is not among the least of the merits of the man that by his sturdy personality, as well as by his unyielding persistence, he won the boy over to the passive admission that there might be something in it. It had not been his experience.

There was the law which sternly commanded him to go to school, and which he laughed at every day. Then there was the law to prevent child labor. It cost twenty-five cents for a false age certificate to break that, and Jacob, if he thought of it at all, probably thought of perjury as rather an expensive thing. A quarter was a good deal to pay for the right to lock a child up in a factory, when he ought to have been at play. The excise law was everybody's game. The sign that hung in every saloon, saying that nothing was sold there to minors, never yet barred out his "growler" when he had the price. There was another such sign in the tobacco shop, forbidding the sale of cigarettes to boys of his age. Jacob calculated that when he had the money he smoked as many as fifteen in a day, and he laughed when he told me. He laughed, too, when he remembered how the boys of the East Side took to carrying balls of cord in their pockets, on the wave of the Lexow reform, on purpose to measure the distance from the school door to the nearest saloon. They had been told that it should be two hundred feet, according to law. There were schools that had as many as a dozen within the tabooed limits. It was in the papers how, when the highest courts said that the law was good, the saloon keepers attacked the schools as a nuisance and detrimental to property. In a general way Jacob sided with the saloon keeper; not because he had any opinion about it, but because it seemed natural. Such opinions as he ordinarily had he got from that quarter.

When, later on, he came to be tried, his counsel said to me, "He is an amazing liar." No, hardly amazing. It would have been amazing if he had been anything else. Lying and mockery were all around him, and he adjusted himself to the things that were. He lied in self-defense.

Jacob's story ends here, as far as he is personally concerned. The story of the gang begins. So trained for the responsibility of citizenship, robbed of home and of childhood, with every prop knocked from under him, all the elements that make for strength and character trodden out in the making of the boy, all the high ambition of youth caricatured by the slum and become base passions,--so equipped he comes to the business of life. As a "kid" he hunted with the pack in the street. As a young man he trains with the gang, because it furnishes the means of gratifying his inordinate vanity, that is the slum's counterfeit of self-esteem. Upon the Jacobs of other days there was a last hold,--the father's authority. Changed conditions have loosened that also. There is a time in every young man's life when he knows more than his father. It is like the measles or the mumps, and he gets over it, with a little judicious firmness in the hand that guides. It is the misfortune of the slum boy of to-day that it is really so, and that he knows it. His father is an Italian or a Jew, and cannot even speak the language to which the boy is born. He has to depend on him in much, in the new order of things. The old man is "slow," he is "Dutch." He maybe an Irishman with some advantages; he is still a "foreigner." He loses his grip on the boy. Ethical standards of which he has no conception clash. Watch the meeting of two currents in river or bay, and see the line of drift that tells of the struggle. So in the city's life strive the currents of the old and the new, and in the churning the boy goes adrift. The last hold upon him is gone. That is why the gang appears in the second generation, the first born upon the soil,--a fighting gang if the Irishman is there with his ready fist, a thievish gang if it is the East Side Jew,--and disappears in the third. The second boy's father is not "slow." He has had experience. He was clubbed into decency in his own day, and the night stick wore off the glamour of the thing. His grip on the boy is good, and it holds.

It depends now upon chance what is to become of the lad. But the slum has stacked the cards against him. There arises in the lawless crowd a leader, who rules with his stronger fists or his readier wit. Around him the gang crystallizes, and what he is it becomes. He may be a thief, like David Meyer, a report of whose doings I have before me. He was just a bully, and, being the biggest in his gang, made the others steal for him and surrender the "swag," or take a licking. But that was unusual. Ordinarily the risk and the "swag" are distributed on more democratic principles. Or he may be of the temper of Mike of Poverty Gap, who was hanged for murder at nineteen. While he sat in his cell at police headquarters, he told with grim humor of the raids of his gang on Saturday nights when they stocked up at "the club." They used to "hook" a butcher's cart or other light wagon, wherever found, and drive like mad up and down the avenue, stopping at saloon or grocery to throw in what they wanted. His job was to sit at the tail of the cart with a six-shooter and pop at any chance pursuer. He chuckled at the recollection of how men fell over one another to get out of his way. "It was great to see them run," he said. Mike was a tough, but with a better chance he might have been a hero. The thought came to him, too, when it was all over and the end in sight. He put it all in one sober, retrospective sigh, that had in it no craven shirking of the responsibility that was properly his: "I never had no bringing up."

There was a meeting some time after his death to boom a scheme for "getting the boys off the street," and I happened to speak of Mike's case. In the audience was a gentleman of means and position, and his daughter, who manifested great interest and joined heartily in the proposed movement. A week later, I was thunderstruck at reading of the arrest of my sympathetic friend's son for train-wrecking up the State. The fellow was of the same age as Mike. It appeared that he was supposed to be attending school, but had been reading dime novels instead, until he arrived at the point where he "had to kill some one before the end of the month." To that end he organized a gang of admiring but less resourceful comrades. After all, the plane of fellowship of Poverty Gap and Madison Avenue lies nearer than we often suppose. I set the incident down in justice to the memory of my friend Mike. If this one went astray with so much to pull him the right way, and but the single strand broken, what then of the other?

Mike's was the day of Irish heroics. Since their scene was shifted from the East Side there has come over there an epidemic of child crime of meaner sort, but following the same principle of gang organization. It is difficult to ascertain the exact extent of it, because of the well-meant but, I am inclined to think, mistaken effort on the part of the children's societies to suppress the record of it for the sake of the boy. Enough testimony comes from the police and the courts, however, to make it clear that thieving is largely on the increase among the East Side boys. And it is amazing at what an early age it begins. When, in the fight for a truant school, I had occasion to gather statistics upon this subject, to meet the sneer of the educational authorities that the "crimes" of street boys compassed at worst the theft of a top or a marble. I found among 278 prisoners, of whom I had kept the run for ten months, two boys, of four and eight years respectively, arrested for breaking into a grocery, not to get candy or prunes, but to rob the till. The little one was useful to "crawl through a small hole." There were "burglars" of six and seven years, and five in a bunch, the whole gang apparently, at the age of eight. "Wild" boys began to appear in court at that age. At eleven, I had seven thieves, two of whom had a record on the police blotter, and an "habitual liar;" at twelve, I had four burglars, three ordinary thieves, two arrested for drunkenness, three for assault, and three incendiaries; at thirteen, five burglars, one with a "record," as many thieves, one "drunk," five charged with assault and one with forgery; at fourteen, eleven thieves and house-breakers, six highway robbers,--the gang on its unlucky day, perhaps,--and ten arrested for fighting, not counting one who had assaulted a policeman, in a state of drunken frenzy. One of the gangs made a specialty of stealing baby carriages, when left unattended in front of stores. They "drapped the kids in the hallway" and "sneaked" the carriages. And so on. The recital was not a pleasant one, but it was effective. We got our truant school, and one way that led to the jail was blocked.

It may be that the leader is neither thief nor thug, but ambitious. In that case the gang is headed for politics by the shortest route. Likewise, sometimes, when he is both. In either case it carries the situation by assault. When the gang wants a thing, the easiest way seems to it always to take it. There was an explosion in a Fifth Street tenement, one night last January, that threw twenty families into a wild panic, and injured two of the tenants badly. There was much mystery about it, until it came out that the housekeeper had had a "run in" with the gang in the block. It wanted club-room in the house, and she would not let it in. Beaten, it avenged itself in characteristic fashion by leaving a package of gunpowder on the stairs, where she would be sure to find it when she went the rounds with her candle to close up. That was a gang of that kind, headed straight for Albany. And what is more, it will get there, unless things change greatly. The gunpowder was just a "bluff" to frighten the housekeeper, an installment of the kind of politics it meant to play when it got its chance. There was "nothing against this gang" except a probable row with the saloon keeper, since it applied elsewhere for house-room. Not every gang has a police record of theft and "slugging" beyond the early encounters of the street. "Our honored leader" is not always the captain of a band of cutthroats. He is the honorary president of the "social club" that bears his name, and he counts for something in the ward. But the ethical standards do not differ. "Do others, or they will do you," felicitously adapted from Holy Writ for the use of the slum, and the classic war-cry, "To the victors the spoils," made over locally to read, "I am not in politics for my health," still interpret the creed of the political as of the "slugging" gang. They drew their inspiration from the same source. Of what gang politics means every large city in our country has had its experience. New York is no exception. History on the subject is being made yet, in the sight of us all.

Our business with the gang, however, is in the making of it. Take now the showing of the reformatory,[4] to which I have before made reference, and see what light it throws upon the matter: 71 per cent. of prisoners with no moral sense, or next to none, yet more than that proportion possessed of "natural mental capacity," which is to say that they had the means of absorbing it from their environment, if there had been any to absorb. Bad homes sent half of all prisoners there; bad company 92 per cent. The reformatory repeats the prison chaplain's verdict, "weakness, not wickedness," in its own way: "Malevolence does not characterize the criminal, but aversion to continuous labor." If "the street" had been written across it in capital letters, it could not have been made plainer. Twelve per cent. only of the prisoners came from good homes, and one in a hundred had kept good company; evidently he was not of the mentally capable. They will tell you at the prison that, under its discipline, 83 per cent. are set upon their feet and make a fresh start. With due allowance for a friendly critic, there is still room for the three fourths labeled normal. The Children's Aid Society will give you even better news of the boys rescued from the slum before it had branded them for its own. Scarce five per cent. are lost, though they leave such a black mark that they make trouble for all the good boys that are sent out from New York. Better than these was the kindergarten record in San Francisco. New York has no monopoly of the slum. Of nine thousand children from the slummiest quarters of that city who had gone through the Golden Gate Association's kindergartens, just one was said to have got into jail. The merchants who looked coldly on the experiment before brought their gold to pay for keeping it up. They were hard-headed men of business, and the demonstration that schools were better than jails any day appealed to them as eminently sane and practical.

[Footnote 4: Year-Book of Elmira State Reformatory, 1897. The statistics deal with 8319 prisoners received there in twenty-three years. The social stratum whence they came is sufficiently indicated by the statement that 18.3 per cent. were illiterates, and 43.3 per cent. were able to read and write with difficulty; 35.2 per cent. had an ordinary common school education; 3.2 per cent. came out of high schools or colleges.]

And well it might. The gang is a distemper of the slum that writes upon the generation it plagues the recipe for its own corrective. It is not the night stick, though in the acute stage that is not to be dispensed with. Neither is it the jail. To put the gang behind iron bars affords passing relief, but it is like treating a symptom without getting at the root of the disease. Prophylactic treatment is clearly indicated. The boy who flings mud and stones is entering his protest in his own way against the purblind policy that gave him jails for schools and the gutter for a playground, that gave him dummies for laws and the tenement for a home. He is demanding his rights, of which he has been cheated,--the right to his childhood, the right to know the true dignity of labor that makes a self-respecting manhood. The gang, rightly understood, is our ally, not our enemy. Like any ailment of the body, it is a friend come to tell us of something that has gone amiss. The thing for us to do is to find out what it is, and set it right.

That is the story of the gang. That we have read and grasped its lesson at last, an item in my morning paper, which I read at the breakfast table to-day, bears witness. It tells that the League for Political Education has set about providing a playground for the children up on the West Side, near the model tenements which I described. Just so! With a decent home and a chance for the boy to grow into a healthy man, his political education can proceed without much further hindrance. Now let the League for Political Education trade off the policeman's club for a boys' club, and it may consider its course fairly organized.

I spoke of the instinct for the crowd in the tenement house boy as evidence that the slum had got its grip on him. And it is true of him. The experience that the helpless poor will not leave their slum when a chance of better things is offered is wearily familiar to most of us. I recall the indignant amazement of my good friend, the president of the Baron de Hirsch Fund, when, of a hundred of the neediest families chosen to be the pioneers in the experiment of transplanting the crowds of the Ghetto to the country, where homes and work were waiting for them, only seven wanted to go. They preferred the excitement of the street. One has to have resources to face the loneliness of the woods and the fields. We have seen what resources the slum has at its command. In the boy it laid hold of the instinct for organization, the desire to fall in and march in line that belongs to all boys, and is not here, as abroad, cloyed with military service in the young years,-- and anyhow is stronger in the American boy than in his European brother,-- and perverted it to its own use. That is the simple secret of the success of the club, the brigade, in winning back the boy. It is fighting the street with its own weapon. The gang is the club run wild.

How readily it owns the kinship was never better shown than by the experience of the College Settlement girls, when they first went to make friends in the East Side tenements. I have told it before, but it will bear telling again, for it holds the key to the whole business. They gathered in the drift, all the little embryo gangs that were tuning up in the district, and made them into clubs,--Young Heroes, Knights of the Round Table, and such like; all except one, the oldest, that had begun to make a name for itself with the police. That one held aloof, observing coldly what went on, to make sure it was "straight." They let it be, keeping the while an anxious eye upon it; until one day there came a delegation with the proposition, "If you will let us in, we will change and have your kind of a gang." Needless to say it was let in. And within a year, when, through a false rumor that the concern was moving away, there was a run on the Settlement's penny provident bank, the converted gang proved itself its stanchest friend by doing actually what John

Halifax did, in Miss Mulock's story: it brought all the pennies it could raise in the neighborhood by hook or by crook and deposited them as fast as the regular patrons--the gang had not yet risen to the dignity of a bank account-- drew them out, until the run ceased.

The cry "Get the boys off the street" that has been raised in our cities, as the real gravity of the situation has been made clear, has led to the adoption of curfew ordinances in many places. Any attempt to fit such a scheme to metropolitan life would probably result simply in adding one more dead- letter law, more dangerous than all the rest, to those we have. Besides, the curfew rings at nine o'clock. The dangerous hours, when the gang is made, are from seven to nine, between supper and bedtime. This is the gap the club fills out. The boys take to the street because the home has nothing to keep them there. To lock them up in the house would only make them hate it more. The club follows the line of least resistance. It has only to keep also on the line of common sense. It must be a real club, not a reformatory. Its proper function is to head off the jail. The gang must not run it. But rather that than have it help train up a band of wretched young cads. The signs are not hard to make out. When a boy has had his head swelled by his importance as a member of the Junior Street-Cleaning Band to the point of reproving his mother for throwing a banana peel in the street, the thing to be done is to take him out and spank him, if it is reverting to "the savagery" of the street. Better a savage than a cad. The boys have the making of both in them. Their vanity furnishes abundant material for the cad, but only when unduly pampered. Left to itself, the gang can be trusted not to develop that kink.

It comes down in the end to the personal influence that is always most potent in dealing with these problems. We had a gang start up once when my boys were of that age, out in the village on Long Island where we lived. It had its headquarters in our barn, where it planned divers raids that aimed at killing the cat and other like outrages; the central fact being that the boys had an air rifle, with which it was necessary to murder something. My wife discovered the conspiracy, and, with woman's wit, defeated it by joining the gang. She "gave in wood" to the election bonfires, and pulled the safety valve upon all the other plots by entering into the true spirit of them,--which was adventure rather than mischief,--and so keeping them within safe lines. She was elected an honorary member, and became the counselor of the gang in all their little scrapes. I can yet see her dear brow wrinkled in the study of some knotty gang problem, which we discussed when the boys had been long asleep. They did not dream of it, and the village never knew what small tragedies it escaped, nor who it was that so skillfully averted them.

It is always the women who do those things. They are the law and the gospel to the boy, both in one. It is the mother heart, I suppose, and there is nothing better in all the world. I am reminded of the conversion of "the Kid" by one who was in a very real sense the mother of a social settlement uptown, in the latitude of Battle Row. The Kid was driftwood. He had been cast off by a drunken father and mother, and was living on what he could scrape out of ash barrels, and an occasional dime for kindling-wood which he sold from a wheel-barrow, when the gang found and adopted him. My friend adopted the gang in her turn, and civilized it by slow stages. Easter Sunday came, when she was to redeem her promise to take the boys to witness the services in a neighboring church, where the liturgy was especially impressive. It found the larger part of the gang at her door,--a minority, it was announced, were out stealing potatoes, hence were excusable,--in a state of high indignation.

"The Kid's been cussin' awful," explained the leader. The Kid showed in the turbulent distance, red-eyed and raging.

"But why?" asked my friend, in amazement.

"'Cause he can't go to church!"

It appeared that the gang had shut him out, with a sense of what was due to the occasion, because of his rags. Restored to grace, and choking down reminiscent sobs, the Kid sat through the Easter service, surrounded by the twenty-seven "proper" members of the gang. Civilization had achieved a victory, and no doubt my friend remembered it in her prayers with thanksgiving. The manner was of less account. Battle Row has its own ways, even in its acceptance of means of grace.

I walked home from the office to-night. The street wore its normal aspect of mingled dullness and the kind of expectancy that is always waiting to turn any excitement, from a fallen horse to a fire, to instant account. The early June heat had driven the multitudes from the tenements into the street for a breath of air. The boys of the block were holding a meeting at the hydrant. In some way they had turned the water on, and were splashing in it with bare feet, reveling in the sense that they were doing something that "went against" their enemy, the policeman. Upon the quiet of the evening broke a bugle note and the tramp of many feet keeping time. A military band came around the corner, stepping briskly to the tune of "The Stars and Stripes Forever." Their white duck trousers glimmered in the twilight, as the hundred legs moved as one. Stoops and hydrant were deserted with a rush. The gang fell in with joyous shouts. The young fellow linked arms with his sweetheart and fell in too. The tired mother hurried with the baby carriage to catch up. The butcher came, hot and wiping his hands on his apron, to the door to see them pass.

"Yes," said my companion, guessing my thoughts,--we had been speaking of the boys,--"but look at the other side. There is the military spirit. Do you not fear danger from it in this country?"

No, my anxious friend, I do not. Let them march; and if with a gun, better still. Often enough it is the choice of the gun on the shoulder, or, by and by, the stripes on the back in the lockstep gang.

VI

LETTING IN THE LIGHT

I had been out of town and my way had not fallen through the Mulberry Bend in weeks until that morning when I came suddenly upon the park that had been made there in my absence. Sod had been laid, and men were going over the lawn cutting the grass after the rain. The sun shone upon flowers and the tender leaves of young shrubs, and the smell of new-mown hay was in the air. Crowds of little Italian children shouted with delight over the "garden," while their elders sat around upon the benches with a look of contentment such as I had not seen before in that place. I stood and looked at it all, and a lump came in my throat as I thought of what it had been, and of all the weary years of battling for this. It had been such a hard fight, and now at last it was won. To me the whole battle with the slum had summed itself up in the struggle with this dark spot. The whir of the lawn mower was as sweet a song in my ear as that which the skylark sang when I was a boy, in

Danish fields, and which gray hairs do not make the man forget.

In my delight I walked upon the grass. It seemed as if I should never be satisfied till I had felt the sod under my feet,--sod in the Mulberry Bend! I did not see the gray-coated policeman hastening my way, nor the wide-eyed youngsters awaiting with shuddering delight the catastrophe that was coming, until I felt his cane laid smartly across my back and heard his angry command:--

"Hey! Come off the grass! D' ye think it is made to walk on?"

So that was what I got for it. It is the way of the world. But it was all right. The park was there, that was the thing. And I had my revenge. I had just had a hand in marking five blocks of tenements for destruction to let in more light, and in driving the slum from two other strongholds. Where they were, parks are being made to-day in which the sign "Keep off the grass!" will never be seen. The children may walk in them from morning till night, and I too, if I want to, with no policeman to drive us off. I tried to tell the policeman something about it. But he was of the old dispensation. All the answer I got was a gruff:--

"G'wan now! I don't want none o' yer guff!"

It was all "guff" to the politicians, I suppose, from the day the trouble began about the Mulberry Bend, but toward the end they woke up nobly. When the park was finally dedicated to the people's use, they took charge of the celebration with immense unction, and invited themselves to sit in the high seats and glory in the achievement which they had done little but hamper and delay from the first. They had not reckoned with Colonel Waring, however. When they had had their say, the colonel arose and, curtly reminding them that they had really had no hand in the business, proposed three cheers for the citizen effort that had struck the slum this staggering blow. There was rather a feeble response on the platform, but rousing cheers from the crowd, with whom the colonel was a prime favorite, and no wonder. Two years later he laid down his life in the fight which he so valiantly and successfully waged. It is the simple truth that he was killed by politics. The services which he had rendered the city would have entitled him in any reputable business to be retained in the employment that was his life and his pride. Had he been so retained he would not have gone to Cuba, and would in all human probability be now alive. But Tammany is not "in politics for her health" and had no use for him, though no more grievous charge could be laid at his door, even in the heat of the campaign, than that he was a "foreigner," being from Rhode Island. Spoils politics never craved a heavier sacrifice of any community.

It was Colonel Waring's broom that first let light into the slum. That which had come to be considered an impossible task he did by the simple formula of "putting a man instead of a voter behind every broom." The words are his own. The man, from a political dummy who loathed his job and himself in it with cause, became a self-respecting citizen, and the streets that had been dirty were swept. The ash barrels which had befouled the sidewalks disappeared, almost without any one knowing it till they were gone. The trucks that obstructed the children's only playground, the street, went with the dirt despite the opposition of the truckman who had traded off his vote to Tammany in the past for stall room at the curbstone. They did not go without a struggle. When appeal to the alderman proved useless, the truckman resorted to strategy. He took a wheel off, or kept a perishing nag, that could not walk, hitched to the truck over night to make it appear that it was there for business. But subterfuge availed as little as resistance. In the Mulberry Bend he made his last stand. The old houses had been torn down, leaving a three-acre lot full of dirt mounds and cellar holes. Into this the truckmen of the Sixth Ward hauled their carts, and defied the street cleaners. They were no longer in their way, and they were on the Park Department's domain, where no Colonel Waring was in control. But while their owners were triumphing, the children playing among the trucks set one of them rolling down into a cellar, and three or four of the little ones were crushed. That was the end. The trucks disappeared. Even Tammany has not ventured to put them back, so great was the relief of their going. They were not only a hindrance to the sweeper and the skulking places of all manner of mischief at night, but I have repeatedly seen the firemen baffled in their efforts to reach a burning house, where they stood four and six deep in the wide "slips" at the river.

Colonel Waring did more for the cause of labor than all the walking delegates of the town together, by investing a despised but highly important task with a dignity which won the hearty plaudits of a grateful city. When he uniformed his men and announced that he was going to parade with them so that we might all see what they were like, the town laughed and poked fun at the "white wings;" but no one went to see them who did not come away converted to an enthusiastic belief in the man and his work. Public sentiment, that had been half reluctantly suspending judgment, expecting every day to see the colonel "knuckle down to politics" like his predecessors, turned in an hour, and after that there was little trouble. The tenement house children organized street cleaning bands to help along the work, and Colonel Waring enlisted them as regular auxiliaries and made them useful.

They had no better friend. When the unhappy plight of the persecuted pushcart men, all immigrant Jews, who were blackmailed, robbed, and driven from pillar to post as a nuisance, though licensed to trade in the street, appealed vainly for a remedy, Colonel Waring found a way out in a great morning market in Hester Street that should be turned over to the children for a playground in the afternoon. Though he proved that it would pay interest on the investment in market fees, and many times in the children's happiness, it was never built. It would have been a most fitting monument to the man's memory. His broom saved more lives in the crowded tenements than a squad of doctors. It did more: it swept the cobwebs out of our civic brain and conscience, and set up a standard of a citizen's duty which, however we may for the moment forget, will be ours until we have dragged other things than our pavements out of the mud.

Even the colonel's broom would have been powerless to do that for "the Bend." That was hopeless and had to go. There was no question of children or playground involved. The worst of all the gangs, the Why, had its headquarters in the darkest of its dark alleys; but it was left to the police. We had not begun to understand that the gangs meant something to us beyond murder and vengeance, in those days. No one suspected that they had any such roots in the soil that they could be killed by merely destroying the slum. The cholera was rapping on our door and, with the Bend there, we felt about it as a man with stolen goods in his house must feel when the policeman comes up the street. Back in the seventies we began discussing what ought to be done. By 1884 the first Tenement House Commission had summoned up courage to propose that a street be cut through the bad block. In the following year a bill was brought in to destroy it bodily, and then began the long fight that resulted in the defeat of the slum a dozen years later.

It was a bitter fight, in which every position of the enemy had to be carried by assault. The enemy was the deadly official inertia that was the outcome of political corruption born of the slum plus the indifference of the mass of our citizens, who probably had never seen the Bend. If I made it my own concern to the exclusion of all else, it was only because I knew it. I had been part of it. Homeless and alone, I had sought its shelter, not for long,--that was not to be endured,--but long enough to taste of its poison, and I hated it. I knew that the blow must be struck there, to kill. Looking back now over those years, I can see that it was all as it should be. We were learning the alphabet of our lesson then. We could have learned it in no other way so thoroughly. Before we had been at it more than two or three years, it was no longer a question of the Bend merely. The Small Parks law that gave us a million dollars a year to force light and air into the slum, to its destruction, grew out of it. The whole sentiment which in its day, groping blindly and angrily, had wiped out the disgrace of the Five Points, just around the corner, crystallized and took shape in its fight. It waited merely for the issue of that, to attack the slum in its other strongholds; and no sooner was the Bend gone than the rest surrendered, unconditionally.

But it was not so easy campaigning at the start. In 1888 plans were filed for the demolition of the block. It took four years to get a report of what it would cost to tear it down. About once in two months during all that time the authorities had to be prodded into a spasm of activity, or we would probably have been yet where we were then. Once when I appealed to the Corporation Counsel to give a good reason for the delay, I got the truth out of him without evasion.

"Well, I tell you," he said blandly, "no one here is taking any interest in that business. That is good enough reason for you, isn't it?"

It was. That Tammany reason became the slogan of an assault upon official incompetence and treachery that hurried things up considerably. The property was condemned at a total cost to the city of a million and a half, in round numbers, including the assessment of half a million for park benefit which the property owners were quick enough, with the aid of the politicians, to get saddled on the city at large. In 1894 the city took possession and became the landlord of the old barracks. For a whole year it complacently collected the rents and did nothing. When it was shamed out of that rut, too, and the tenements were at last torn down, the square lay as the wreckers had left it for another year, until it became such a plague spot that, as a last resort, with a citizen's privilege, I arraigned the municipality before the Board of Health for maintaining a nuisance upon its premises. I can see the shocked look of the official now, as he studied the complaint.

"But, my dear sir," he coughed diplomatically, "isn't it rather unusual? I never heard of such a thing."

"Neither did I," I replied, "but then there never was such a thing before."

That night, while they were debating the "unusual thing," happened the accident to the children of which I spoke, emphasizing the charge that the nuisance was "dangerous to life," and there was an end. In the morning the Bend was taken in hand, and the following spring the Mulberry Bend Park was opened.

A million dollars a year had been lost while we were learning our lesson. The Small Parks Fund was not cumulative, and when it came to paying for the Bend a special bill had to be passed to authorize it, the award being "more than one million in one year." The wise financiers who framed and hung in the comptroller's office a check for three cents that had been under-paid on a school site, for the taxpayer to bow before in awe and admiration at such business methods, could find no way to make the appropriation for two years apply, though the new year was coming in a week or two. But the Gilder Tenement House Commission had been sitting, the Committee of Seventy had been at work, and a law was on the statute books authorizing the expenditure of three million dollars for two open spaces in the parkless district on the East Side, where Jacob Beresheim was born. It had shown that while the proportion of park area inside the limits of the old city was equal to one thirteenth of all, below Fourteenth Street, where one third of the people lived, it was barely one fortieth. It took a citizen's committee appointed by the mayor just three weeks to seize the two sites which are now being laid out in playgrounds chiefly, and it took the Good Government Clubs with their allies at Albany less than two months to get warrant of law for the tearing down of the houses ahead of final condemnation lest any mischance befall through delay or otherwise,--a precaution which subsequent events proved to be eminently wise. The slow legal proceedings are going on yet.

[Illustration: MULBERRY BEND PARK]

The playground part of it was a provision of the Gilder law that showed what apt scholars we had been. I was a member of that committee, and I fed fat my grudge against the slum tenement, knowing that I might not again have such a chance. Bone Alley went. I shall not soon get the picture of it, as I saw it last, out of my mind. I had wandered to the top floor of one of the ramshackle tenements in the heart of the block, to a door that stood ajar, and pushed it open. On the floor lay three women rag-pickers with their burdens, asleep, overcome by the heat and the beer, the stale stench of which filled the place. Swarms of flies covered them. The room--no! let it go. Thank God, we shall not again hear of Bone Alley. Where it stood workmen are to-day building a gymnasium with baths for the people, and a playground and park which may even be turned into a skating-pond in winter if the architect keeps his promise. A skating-pond for the children of the Eleventh Ward! No wonder the politician is in a hurry to take the credit for what is going forward over there. It is that or nothing with him now. It will be all up with Tammany, once the boys find out that these were the things she withheld from them all the years, for her own gain.

Half a dozen blocks away the city's first public bath house is at last going up, after many delays, and godliness will have a chance to move in with cleanliness. The two are neighbors everywhere, but in the slum the last must come first. Glasgow has half a dozen public baths. Rome, two thousand years ago, washed its people most sedulously, and in heathen Japan to-day, I am told, there are baths, as we have saloons, on every corner. Christian New York never had a bath house. In a tenement population of 255,033 the Gilder Committee found only 306 who had access to bath-rooms in the houses where they lived. The Church Federation canvass of the Fifteenth Assembly District counted three bath-tubs to 1321 families. Nor was that because they so elected. The People's Baths took in 115,000 half dimes last year for as many baths, and forty per cent. of their customers were Italians. The free river baths admitted 5,096,876 customers during the summer. The "great unwashed" were not so from choice, it would appear.

Bone Alley brought thirty-seven dollars under the auctioneer's hammer.

Thieves' Alley, in the other park down at Rutgers Square, where the police clubbed the Jewish cloakmakers a few years ago for the offense of gathering to assert their right to "being men, live the life of men," as some one who knew summed up the labor movement, brought only seven dollars, and the old Helvetia House, where Boss Tweed and his gang met at night to plan their plundering raids on the city's treasury, was knocked down for five. Kerosene Row would not have brought enough to buy kindling wood with which to start one of the numerous fires that gave it its bad name. It was in Thieves' Alley that the owner in the days long gone by hung out the sign: "No Jews need apply." Last week I watched the opening of the first municipal playground upon the site of the old alley, and in the thousands that thronged street and tenements from curb to roof with thunder of applause, there were not twoscore who could have found lodging with the old Jew-baiter. He had to go with his alley before the better day could bring light and hope to the Tenth Ward.

In all this the question of rehousing the population, that had to be so carefully considered abroad in the destruction of slums, gave no trouble. The speculative builder had seen to that. In the five wards, the Seventh, Tenth, Eleventh, Thirteenth, and Seventeenth, in which the unhoused ones would look for room, if they wanted to stay near their old home, there were, according to the tenement census at the time when the old houses were torn down, 4268 vacant apartments, with room for more than 18,000 persons at our average of four and a half to the family. Even including the Mulberry Bend, the whole number of the dispossessed was not 10,000. On Manhattan Island there were at this time more than 37,000 vacant apartments, so that the question could not arise in any serious shape, much as it plagued the dreams of some well-meaning people. As a matter of fact the unhoused were scattered much more widely than had been anticipated, which was one of the very purposes sought to be attained. Many of them had remained in their old slum more from force of habit and association than because of necessity.

"Everything takes ten years," said Abram S. Hewitt when, exactly ten years after he had as mayor championed the Small Parks Act, he took his seat as chairman of the Advisory Committee on Small Parks. The ten years had wrought a great change. It was no longer the slum of to-day, but that of to-morrow that challenged attention. The committee took the point of view of the children from the first. It had a large map prepared showing where in the city there was room to play and where there was none. Then it called in the police and asked them to point out where there was trouble with the boys; and in every instance the policeman put his finger upon a treeless slum.

"They have no other playground than the street," was the explanation given in each case. "They smash lamps and break windows. The storekeepers kick and there is trouble. That is how it begins." "Many complaints are received daily of boys annoying pedestrians, storekeepers, and tenants by their continually playing baseball in some parts of almost every street. The damage is not slight. Arrests are frequent, much more frequent than when they had open lots to play in." This last was the report of an uptown captain. He remembered the days when there were open lots there. "But these lots are now built upon," he said, "and for every new house there are more boys and less chance for them to play."

The committee put a red daub on the map to indicate trouble. Then it asked those police captains who had not spoken to show them where their precincts were, and why they had no trouble. Every one of them put his finger on a green spot that marked a park. "My people are quiet and orderly," said the captain of the Tompkins Square precinct. The police took the square from a mob by storm twice in my recollection, and the commander of the precinct then was hit on the head with a hammer by "his people" and laid out for dead. "The Hook Gang is gone," said he of Corlears Hook. The professional pursuit of that gang was to rob and murder inoffensive citizens by night and throw them into the river, and it achieved a bad eminence at its calling. "The whole neighborhood has taken a change, and decidedly for the better," said the captain of Mulberry Street, and the committee rose and said that it had heard enough.

The map was hung on the wall, and in it were stuck pins to mark the site of present and projected schools as showing where the census had found the children crowding. The moment that was done the committee sent the map and a copy of chapter 338 of the laws of 1895 to the mayor, and reported that its task was finished. This is the law and all there is of it:--

"The people of the State of New York, represented in Senate and Assembly, do enact as follows:--

"Section 1. Hereafter no schoolhouse shall be constructed in the city of New York without an open-air playground attached to or used in connection with the same.

"Section 2. This act shall take effect immediately."

Where the map was daubed with red the school pins crowded one another. On the lower East Side, where child crime was growing fast, and no less than three storm centres were marked down by the police, nine new schools were going up or planned, and in the uptown precinct whence came the wail about the ball players there were seven. The playground had proved its case. Where it was expedient it was to be a school playground. It seemed a happy combination, for the new law had been a stumbling-block to the school commissioners, who were in a quandary over the needful size of an "open-air playground." The success of the roof-garden idea suggested a way out. But schools are closed at the time of the year when playgrounds are most needed for city children. To get the garden on the roof of the schoolhouse recognized as the public playground seemed a long step toward turning it into a general neighborhood evening resort that should be always open, and so toward bringing school and people, and especially the school and the boy, together in a bond of mutual sympathy highly desirable for both.

That was the burden of the committee's report. It made thirteen recommendations besides, as to the location of parks and detached playgrounds, only one of which has been adopted. But that is of less account--as also was the information imparted to me as secretary of the committee by our peppery Tammany mayor, that we had "as much authority as a committee of bootblacks in his office"--than the fact that the field has at last been studied and its needs have been made known. The rest will follow, with or without the politician's authority. The one recommendation that has been carried out was that of a riverside park in the region uptown on the West Side where the Federation of Churches and Christian Workers found "saloon social ideals minting themselves upon the minds of the people at the rate of seven saloon thoughts to one educational thought." There is an outdoor gymnasium to-day on the chosen site,--while the legal proceedings to take possession are unraveling their red tape,--and a recreation pier hard by. In the evening the young men of the neighborhood may be seen trooping riverward with their girls to hear the music. The gang that "laid out" two policemen, to my knowledge, has gone out of business.

The best laid plans are sometimes upset by surprising snags. We had planned for two municipal playgrounds on the East Side where the need is greatest, and our plans were eagerly accepted by the city authorities. But they were never put into practice. A negligent attorney killed one, a lazy clerk the other. And both served under the reform government. The first of the two playgrounds was to have been in Rivington Street, adjoining the new public bath, where the boys, for want of something better to do, were fighting daily battles with stones, to the great damage of windows and the worse aggravation of the householders. Four hundred children in that neighborhood petitioned the committee for a place of their own where there were no windows to break, and we found one. It was only after the proceedings had been started that we discovered that they had been taken under the wrong law and the money spent in advertising had been wasted. It was then too late. The daily assaults upon the windows were resumed. The other case was an attempt to establish a model school park in a block where more than four thousand children attended day and night school. The public school and the pro-cathedral, which divided the children between them, were to be allowed to stand, at opposite ends of the block. The surrounding tenements were to be torn down to make room for a park and playground which should embody the ideal of what such a place ought to be, in the opinion of the committee. The roof garden was not in the original plan except as an alternative of the street-level playground, where land came too high. The plentiful supply of light and air, the safety from fire to be obtained by putting the school in a park, beside the fact that it could thus be "built beautiful," were considerations of weight. Plans were made, and there was great rejoicing in Essex Street, until it came out that this scheme had gone the way of the other. The clerk who should have filed the plans in the register's office left that duty to some one else, and it took just twenty-one days to make the journey, a distance of five hundred feet or less. The Greater New York had come then with Tammany, and the thing was not heard of again. When I traced the failure down to the clerk in question, and told him that he had killed the park, he yawned and said:--

"Yes, and I think it is just as well it is dead. We haven't any money for those things. It is very nice to have small parks, and very nice to have a horse and wagon, if you can afford it. But we can't. Why, there isn't money enough to run the city government."

So the labor of weary weeks and months in the children's behalf was all undone by a third-rate clerk in an executive office; but he saved the one thing he had in mind: the city government is "run" to date, and his pay is secure.

Neither stupidity, spite, nor the false cry that "reform extravagance" has wrecked the city's treasury will be able much longer, however, to cheat the child out of his rights. The playground is here to wrestle with the gang for the boy, and it will win. It came so quietly that we hardly knew of it till we heard the shouts. It took us seven years to make up our minds to build a play pier,-- recreation pier is its municipal title,--and it took just about seven weeks to build it when we got so far; but then we learned more in one day than we had dreamed of in the seven years. Half the East Side swarmed over it with shrieks of delight, and carried the mayor and the city government, who had come to see the show, fairly off their feet. And now "we are seven," or will be when the one in Brooklyn has been built,--great, handsome structures, seven hundred feet long, some of them, with music every night for mother and the babies, and for papa, who can smoke his pipe there in peace. The moon shines upon the quiet river, and the steamers go by with their lights. The street is far away with its noise. The young people go sparking in all honor, as it is their right to do. The councilman who spoke the other day of "pernicious influences" lying in wait for them there made the mistake of his life, unless he has made up his mind to go out of politics. The play piers have taken a hold of the people which no crabbed old bachelor can loosen with trumped-up charges. Their civilizing influence upon the children is already felt in a reported demand for more soap in the neighborhood where they are, and even the grocer smiles approval.

The play pier is the kindergarten in the educational campaign against the gang. It gives the little ones a chance. Often enough it is a chance for life. The street as a playground is a heavy contributor to the undertaker's bank account. I kept the police slips of a single day in May two years ago, when four little ones were killed and three crushed under the wheels of trucks in tenement streets. That was unusual, but no day has passed in my recollection that has not had its record of accidents which bring grief as deep and lasting to the humblest home as if it were the pet of some mansion on Fifth Avenue that was slain. The kindergarten teaching bore fruit. To-day there are half a dozen full-blown playgrounds downtown and uptown where the children swarm. Private initiative set the pace, but the idea has been engrafted upon the municipal plan. The city helped get at least one of them under way. The Outdoor Recreation League was organized last year by public-spirited citizens, including many amateur athletes and enthusiastic women, with the object of "obtaining recognition of the necessity for recreation and physical exercise as fundamental to the moral and physical welfare of the people." Together with the Social Reform Club and the Federation of Churches and Christian Workers it maintained a playground on the uptown West Side last summer. The ball came into play there for the first time as a recognized factor in civic progress. The day might well be kept for all time among those that mark human emancipation, for it was social reform and Christian work in one, of the kind that tells.

Only the year before, the athletic clubs had vainly craved the privilege of establishing a gymnasium in the East River Park, where the children wistfully eyed the sacred grass, and cowered under the withering gaze of the policeman. A friend whose house stands opposite the park found them one day swarming over her stoop in such shoals that she could not enter, and asked them why they did not play tag under the trees instead. The instant shout came back: "'Cause the cop won't let us." Now a splendid gymnasium has been opened on the site of the people's park that is to come at Fifty-Third Street and Eleventh Avenue. It is called Hudsonbank. A board fence more than a thousand feet long surrounds it. The director pointed out to me with pride, last week, that not a board had been stolen from it in a year, while other fences within twenty feet of it were ripped to pieces. And he was right. The neighborhood is one that has been anything but distinguished for its respect for private property in the past, and where boards have a market value among the Irish settlers. Better testimony could not have been borne to the spirit in which the gift was accepted by the children.

Poverty Gap, that was fairly transformed by one brief season's experience with its "Holy Terror Park,"[5] a dreary sand lot upon the site of the old tenements in which the Alley Gang once murdered the one good boy of the block for the offense of supporting his aged parents by his work as a baker's apprentice,--Poverty Gap is to have its permanent playground, and Mulberry Bend and Corlears Hook are down on the League's books; which is equivalent to saying that they, too, will shortly know the climbing pole and the vaulting buck. For years the city's only playground that had any claim upon the name-- and that was only a little asphalted strip behind a public school in First Street- -was an old graveyard. We struggled vainly to get possession of another, long abandoned. The dead were of more account than the living. But now at last it is their turn. The other day I watched the children at their play in the new Hester Street gymnasium. The dusty square was jammed with a mighty multitude. It was not an ideal spot, for it had not rained in weeks, and powdered sand and cinders had taken wing and floated like a pall over the perspiring crowd. But it was heaven to them. A hundred men and boys stood in line, waiting their turn upon the bridge ladder and the traveling rings that hung full of struggling and squirming humanity, groping madly for the next grip. No failure, no rebuff discouraged them. Seven boys and girls rode with looks of deep concern--it is their way--upon each end of the see-saw, and two squeezed into each of the forty swings that had room for one, while a hundred counted time and saw that none had too much. It is an article of faith with these children that nothing that is "going" for their benefit is to be missed. Sometimes the result provokes a smile, as when a band of young Jews, starting up a club, called themselves the Christian Heroes. It was meant partly as a compliment, I suppose, to the ladies that gave them club-room; but at the same time, if there was anything in a name, they were bound to have it. It is rather to cry over than to laugh at, if one but understands it. The sight of these little ones swarming over a sand heap until scarcely an inch of it was in sight, and gazing in rapt admiration at the poor show of a dozen geraniums and English ivy plants in pots on the window-sill of the overseer's cottage, was pathetic in the extreme. They stood for ten minutes at a time resting their eyes upon them. In the crowd were aged women and bearded men with the inevitable Sabbath silk hat, who it seemed could never get enough of it. They moved slowly, when crowded out, looking back many times at the enchanted spot, as long as it was in sight.

[Footnote 5: The name was bestowed before the fact, not after.]

Perhaps there was in it, on the part of the children at least, just a little bit of the comforting sense of proprietorship. They had contributed of their scant pennies more than a hundred dollars toward the opening of the playground, and they felt that it was their very own. All the better. Two policemen watched the passing show, grinning. But their clubs hung idly from their belts. The words of a little woman whom I met last year in Chicago kept echoing in my ear. She was the "happiest woman alive," for she had striven long for a playground for her poor children, and had got it.

"The police like it," she said. "They say that it will do more good than all the Sunday schools in Chicago. The mothers say, 'This is good business.' The carpenters that put up the swings and things worked with a will; everybody was glad. The police lieutenant has had a tree called after him. The boys that did that used to be terrors. Now they take care of the trees. They plead for a low limb that is in the way, that no one may cut it off."

The twilight deepens and the gates of the playground are closed. The crowds disperse slowly. In the roof garden on the Hebrew Institute across East Broadway lights are twinkling and the band is tuning up. Little groups are settling down to a quiet game of checkers or love-making. Paterfamilias leans back against the parapet where palms wave luxuriously in the summer breeze. The newspaper drops from his hand; he closes his eyes and is in dreamland, where strikes come not. Mother knits contentedly in her seat, with a smile on her face that was not born of the Ludlow Street tenement. Over yonder a knot of black-browed men talk with serious mien. They might be met any night in the anarchist caf? half a dozen doors away, holding forth against empires. Here wealth does not excite their wrath, nor power their plotting. In the roof garden anarchy is harmless, even though a policeman typifies its government. They laugh pleasantly to one another as he passes, and he gives them a match to light their cigars. It is Thursday, and smoking is permitted. On Friday it is discouraged because it offends the orthodox, to whom the lighting of a fire, even the holding of a candle, is anathema on the Sabbath eve.

The band plays on. One after another, tired heads droop upon babes slumbering peacefully at the breast. Ludlow Street, the tenement, are forgotten; eleven o'clock is not yet. Down along the silver gleam of the river a mighty city slumbers. The great bridge has hung out its string of shining pearls from shore to shore. "Sweet land of liberty!" Overhead the dark sky, the stars that twinkled their message to the shepherds on Judean hills, that lighted their sons through ages of slavery, and the flag of freedom borne upon the breeze,--down there the tenement, the--Ah, well! let us forget, as do these.

Now if you ask me: "And what of it all? What does it avail?" let me take you once more back to the Mulberry Bend, and to the policeman's verdict add the police reporter's story of what has taken place there. In fifteen years I never knew a week to pass without a murder there, rarely a Sunday. It was the wickedest, as it was the foulest, spot in all the city. In the slum the two are interchangeable terms for reasons that are clear enough to me. But I shall not speculate about it, only state the facts. The old houses fairly reeked with outrage and violence. When they were torn down, I counted seventeen deeds of blood in that place which I myself remembered, and those I had forgotten probably numbered seven times seventeen. The district attorney connected more than a score of murders of his own recollection with Bottle Alley, the Why?gang's headquarters. Two years have passed since it was made into a park, and scarce a knife has been drawn, or a shot fired, in all that neighborhood. Only twice have I been called as a police reporter to the spot. It is not that the murder has moved to another neighborhood, for there has been no increase of violence in Little Italy or wherever else the crowd went that moved out. It is that the light has come in and made crime hideous. It is being let in wherever the slum has bred murder and robbery, bred the gang, in the past. Wait, now, another ten years, and let us see what a story there will be to tell.

Avail? Why, here is Tammany actually applauding Comptroller Coler's words in Plymouth Church last night: "Whenever the city builds a schoolhouse upon the site of a dive and creates a park, a distinct and permanent mental, moral, and physical improvement has been made, and public opinion will sustain such a policy, even if a dive-keeper is driven out of business and somebody's ground rent is reduced." And Tammany's press agent sends forth this paen: "In the light of such events how absurd it is for the enemies of the organization to contend that Tammany is not the greatest moral force in the community." Tammany a moral force! The park and the playground have availed, then, to bring back the day of miracles.

VII

JUSTICE FOR THE BOY

Sometimes, when I see my little boy hugging himself with delight at the near prospect of the kindergarten, I go back in memory forty years and more to the day when I was dragged, a howling captive, to school, as a punishment for being bad at home. I remember, as though it were yesterday, my progress up the street in the vengeful grasp of an exasperated servant, and my reception by the aged monster--most fitly named Madame Bruin--who kept the school. She asked no questions, but led me straightway to the cellar, where she plunged me into an empty barrel and put the lid on over me. Applying her horn goggles to the bunghole, to my abject terror, she informed me, in a sepulchral voice, that that was the way bad boys were dealt with in school. When I ceased howling from sheer fright, she took me out and conducted me to the yard, where a big hog had a corner to itself. She bade me observe that one of its ears had been slit half its length. It was because the hog was lazy, and little boys who were that way minded were in danger of similar treatment; in token whereof she clipped a pair of tailor's shears suggestively close to my ear. It was my first lesson in school. I hated it from that hour.

The barrel and the hog were never part of the curriculum in any American boy's school, I suppose; they seem too freakish to be credited to any but the demoniac ingenuity of my home ogre. But they stood for a comprehension of the office of school and teacher which was not patented by any day or land. It is not so long since the notion yet prevailed that the schools were principally to lock children up in for the convenience of their parents, that we should have entirely forgotten it. Only the other day a clergyman from up the State came into my office to tell of a fine reform school they had in his town. They were very proud of it.

"And how about the schools for the good boys in your town?" I asked, when I had heard him out. "Are they anything to be proud of?"

He stared. He guessed they were all right, he said, after some hesitation. But it was clear that he did not know.

It is not necessary to go back forty years to find us in the metropolis upon the clergyman's platform, if not upon Madame Bruin's. Ten will do. They will bring us to the day when roof playgrounds were contemptuously left out of the estimates for an East Side school, as "frills" that had nothing to do with education; when the Board of Health found but a single public school in more than sixscore that was so ventilated as to keep the children from being poisoned by foul air; when the authority of the Talmud had to be invoked by the Superintendent of School Buildings to convince the president of the Board of Education, who happened to be a Jew, that seventy-five or eighty pupils were far too many for one class-room; when a man who had been dead a year was appointed a school trustee of the Third Ward, under the mouldy old law surviving from the day when New York was a big village, and filled the office as well as if he had been alive, because there were no schools in his ward; when manual training and the kindergarten were yet the fads of yesterday, looked at askance; when fifty thousand children roamed the streets for whom there was no room in the schools, and the only defense of the School Commissioners was that they "didn't know" there were so many; and when we mixed truants and thieves in a jail with entire unconcern. Indeed, the jail filled the title role in the educational cast of that day. Its inmates were well lodged and cared for, while the sanitary authorities twice condemned the Essex Market school across the way as wholly unfit for children to be in, but failed to catch the ear of the politician who ran things unhindered. When (in 1894) I denounced the "system" of enforcing--or not enforcing--the compulsory education law as a device to make thieves out of our children by turning over their training to the street, he protested angrily; but the experts of the Tenement House Committee found the charge fully borne out by the facts. They were certainly plain enough in the sight of us all, had we chosen to see.

When at last we saw, we gave the politician a vacation for a season. To say that he was to blame for all the mischief would not be fair. We were to blame for leaving him in possession. He was only a link in the chain which our indifference had forged; but he was always and everywhere an obstruction to betterment,--sometimes, illogically, in spite of himself. Successive Tammany mayors had taken a stand for the public schools, when it was clear that reform could not be delayed much longer; but they were helpless against a system of selfishness and stupidity of which they were the creatures, though they posed as its masters. They had to go with it as unfit, and upon the wave that swept out the last of the rubbish came reform. The Committee of Seventy took hold, the Good Government Clubs, the Tenement House Committee, and the women of New York. Five years we strove with the powers of darkness, and look now at the change. The New York school system is not yet the ideal one,--it may never be; but the jail, at least, has been cast out of the firm. We have a compulsory education law under which it will be possible, when a seat has been provided for every child, to punish the parent for the boy's truancy, unless he surrenders him as unmanageable; and we can count the months now till every child shall find the latchstring out on the school door. We have had to put our hands deep into our pockets to get to that point, but we are nearly there now. Since 1895 the expenditure of twenty-two and a half millions of dollars for new schools in the old city has been authorized by law, and two thirds of the money has been spent. Fifty-odd new buildings have been put up, or are going up while I am writing, every one of them with its playground, which will by and by be free to all the neighborhood. The idea is at last working through that the schools belong to the people, and are primarily for the children and their parents; not mere vehicles of ward patronage, or for keeping an army of teachers in office and pay.

The silly old regime is dead. The ward trustee is gone with his friend the alderman, loudly proclaiming the collapse of our liberties in the day that saw the schools taken from "the people's" control. They were "the people." Experts manage our children's education, which was supposed in the old plan to be the only thing that did not require any training. To superintend a brickyard demanded some knowledge, but anybody could run the public schools. It cost us an election to take that step. One of the Tammany district leaders, who knew what he was talking about, said to me after it was all over: "I knew we would win. Your bringing those foreigners here did the business. Our people believe in home rule. We kept account of the teachers you brought from out of town, and who spent the money they made here out of town, and it got to be the talk among the tenement people in my ward that their daughters would have no more show to get to be teachers. That did the business. We figured the school vote in the city at forty-two thousand, and I knew we could not lose." The "foreigners" were teachers from Massachusetts and other States, who had achieved a national reputation at their work.

There lies upon my table a copy of the minutes of the Board of Education of January 9, 1895, in which is underscored a report on a primary school in the Bronx. "It is a wooden shanty," is the inspector's account, "heated by stoves, and is a regular tinder box; cellar wet, and under one class-room only. This building was erected in order, I believe, to determine whether or not there was a school population in the neighborhood to warrant the purchase of property to erect a school on."

That was the way then of taking a school census, and the result was the utter failure of the compulsory education law to compel anything. To-day we have a biennial census, ordained by law, which, when at last it gets into the hands of some one who can count, will tell us how many Jacob Beresheims are drifting upon the shoals of the street. And we have a truant school to keep them safe in. To it, says the law, no thief shall be committed. It is not yet five years since the burglar and the truant--who, having been refused admission to the school because there was not room for him, inconsequently was locked up for contracting idle ways--were herded in the Juvenile Asylum, and classified there in squads of those who were four feet, four feet seven, and over four feet seven! I am afraid I scandalized some good people, during the fight for decency in this matter, by insisting that it ought to be considered a good mark for Jacob that he despised such schools as were provided for him. But it was true. Except for the risk of the burglar, the jail was preferable by far. A woman has now had charge of the truant school for fourteen months, and she tells me that of quite twenty-five hundred boys scarce sixty were rightly called incorrigible, and even these a little longer and tighter grip would probably win over. For such, a farm school is yet to be provided. The rest responded promptly to an appeal to their pride. She "made it a personal matter" with each of them, and the truant vanished; the boy was restored. The burglar, too, made it a personal matter in the old contact, and the result was two burglars for one. In common with nearly all those who have paid attention to this matter, Mrs. Alger believes that the truant school strikes at the root of the problem of juvenile crime. After thirty years of close acquaintance with the child population of London, Mr. Andrew Drew, chairman of the Industrial Committee of the School Board, declared his conviction that "truancy is to be credited with nearly the whole of our juvenile criminality." But for years there seemed to be no way of convincing the New York School Board that the two had anything to do with each other. As executive officer of the Good Government Clubs, I fought that fight to a finish. We got the school, and in Mrs. Alger, at the time a truant officer, a person singularly well qualified to take charge of it. She has recently been removed, that her place might be given to a man. It is the old scheme come back,--a voter behind the broom,--and the old slough waiting to overwhelm us again.

But it will not get the chance. I have my own idea of how this truancy question is going to be solved. Yesterday I went with Superintendent Snyder through some of the new schools he is building, upon what he calls the letter H plan, in the crowded districts. It is the plan of the H 魁 el de Cluny in Paris, and to my mind as nearly perfect as it is possible to make a schoolhouse. There is not a dark corner in the whole structure, from the splendid gymnasium under the red-tiled roof to the indoor playground on the ground floor, which, when thrown in one with the two open-air playgrounds that lie embraced in the arms of the H, will give the children nearly an acre of asphalted floor space from street to street, to romp on. Seven such schools are going up to-day, each a beautiful palace, and within the year sixteen thousand children will be housed in them. When I think of the old Allen Street school, where the gas had to be kept burning even on the brightest days, recitations suspended every half hour, and the children made to practice calisthenics so that they should not catch cold while the windows were opened to let in fresh air; of the dark playground downstairs, with the rats keeping up such a racket that one could hardly hear himself speak at times, or of the other East Side playground where the boys "weren't allowed to speak above a whisper," so as not to disturb those studying overhead, I fancy that I can make out both the cause and the cure of the boy's desperation. "We try to make our schools pleasant enough to hold the children," wrote the Superintendent of Schools in Indianapolis to me once, and added that they had no truant problem worth bothering about. With the kindergarten and manual training firmly engrafted upon the school course, as they are at last, and with it reaching out to enlist also the boy's play through playground and vacation schools, I shall be willing to turn the boy, who will not come in, over to the reformatory. They will not need to build a new wing to the jail for his safe-keeping.

All ways lead to Rome. The reform in school-building dates back, as does every other reform in New York, to the Mulberry Bend. It began there. The first school that departed from the soulless old tradition, to set beautiful pictures before the child's mind as well as dry figures on the slate, was built there. At the time I wanted it to stand in the park, hoping so to hasten the laying out of that; but although the Small Parks law expressly permitted the erection on park property of buildings for "the instruction of the people," the officials upon whom I pressed my scheme could not be made to understand that as including schools. Perhaps they were right. I catechised thirty-one Fourth Ward girls in a sewing school, about that time, twenty-six of whom had attended the public schools of the district more than a year. One wore a badge earned for excellence in her studies. In those days every street corner was placarded with big posters of Napoleon on a white horse riding through fire and smoke. There was one right across the street. Yet only one of the thirty-one knew who Napoleon was. She "thought she had heard of the gentleman before." It came out that the one impression she retained of what she had heard was that "the gentleman" had two wives. They knew of Washington that he was the first President of the United States, and cut down a cherry-tree. They were sitting and sewing at the time almost on the identical spot where he lived and held office. To the question who ruled before Washington the answer came promptly: no one; he was the first. They agreed reluctantly, upon further consideration, that there was probably "a King of America" before his day, and the Irish damsels turned up their noses at the idea. The people of Canada, they thought, were copper-colored. The same winter I was indignantly bidden to depart from a school in the Fourth Ward by a trustee who had heard that I had written a book about the slum and spoken of "his people" in it.

Those early steps in the reform path stumbled sadly at times over obstacles that showed how dense was the ignorance and how rank were the prejudices we had to fight. When I wrote that the Allen Street school was overrun by rats, which was a fact any one might observe for himself by spending five minutes in the building, I was called sharply to account by the Mayor in the Board of Estimate and Apportionment. There were no rats, he said. The Allen Street school was the worst of them all, and I determined that the time had come to make a demonstration. I procured a rat trap, and was waiting for an idle hour to go over and catch one of the rats, so that I might have it stuffed and sent to the board over which the Mayor presided, as a convincing exhibit; but before I got so far reform swept the whole conspiracy of ignorance and jobbery out of the City Hall.

That was well enough as far as it went; but that the broom was needed elsewhere we learned later, when the Good Government Clubs fought for the inspection of the schools and of the children by trained oculists. The evidence was that the pupils were made both near-sighted and stupid by the want of proper arrangement of their seats and of themselves in the class-room. The fact was not denied, and the scheme was strongly indorsed by the Board of Health and by some of the ablest and best known oculists in the city; but it was wrecked upon an opposition in which we heard the ignorant and selfish cry that it would "interfere with private practice," and so curtail the profits of the practitioner. The proposal to inspect the classes daily for evidence of contagious disease--which, carried out, has proved a most effective means of preventing the spread of epidemics, and one of the greatest blessings--had been opposed, happily unsuccessfully, with the same arguments.[6] It is very well to prate about the rapacity of politicians, but these things came often enough to show what they meant by the claim that they were "closer to the people" than we who were trying to help them; and they were all the more exasperating because they came rarely from below,--the tenement people, when they were not deliberately misled, were ready and eager to fall in with any plan for bettering things, notably where it concerned the schools,--but usually from those who knew better, and from whom we had a right to expect support and backing.

[Footnote 6: I set down reluctantly this censure of an honored profession, to individual members of which I have been wont, in a long succession of troubled years, to go for advice and help in public matters, and never in vain. The statement of the chief sanitary officer of the Health Department, reaffirmed at the time I am writing, is, however, positive to the effect that to this opposition, and this only, was due the failure of that much-needed reform which had for years been with me a pet measure.]

Speaking of that reminds me of a mishap I had in the Hester Street school,-- the one with the "frills" which the Board of Education cut off. I happened to pass it after school hours, and went in to see what sort of a playground the roof would have made. I met no one on the way, and, finding the scuttle open, climbed out and up the slant of the roof to the peak, where I sat musing over our lost chance, when the janitor came to close up. He must have thought I was a crazy man, and my explanation did not make it any better. He haled me down, and but for the fortunate chance that the policeman on the beat knew me, I should have been taken to the lockup as a dangerous lunatic,--all for dreaming of a playground on the roof of a schoolhouse.

Janitor and Board of Commissioners to the contrary notwithstanding, the dream became real. There stands another school in Hester Street to-day within easy call, that has a playground measuring more than twelve thousand square feet on the roof, one of half that size down on the ground, and an asphalted indoor playground as big as the one on the roof. Together they measure a trifle less than thirty thousand feet. To the indignant amazement of my captor, the janitor, his school was thrown open to the children in the last summer vacation, and in the winter they put a boys' club in to worry him. What further indignities there are in store for him, in this day of "frills," there is no telling. A resolution is on record which states, under date of May 18, 1897, that "it is the sense of the Board of Superintendents that the schoolhouses may well be used in the cause of education as neighborhood centres, providing reading-rooms, branch offices of public libraries, etc." And to cut off all chance of relapse into the old doubt whether "such things are educational," that laid so many of our hopes on the dusty shelf of the circumlocution office, the state legislature has expressly declared that the commonwealth will take the chance, which Boards of Education shunned, of a little amusement creeping in. The schools may be used for "purposes of recreation." To the janitor it must seem that the end of all things is at hand.

In the crowded districts, the school playgrounds were thrown open to the children during the long vacation last year, with kindergarten teachers to amuse them, and half a score of vacation schools tempted more than four thousand children from the street into the cool shade of the class-rooms. They wrought in wood and iron, they sang and they played and studied nature,--out of a barrel, to be sure, that came twice a week from Long Island filled with "specimens;" but toward the end we took a hint from Chicago, and let the children gather their own specimens on excursions around the bay and suburbs of the city. That was a tremendous success. The mere hint that money might be lacking to pay for the excursions this summer set the St. Andrew's Brotherhood men on Long Island to devising schemes for inviting the schoolchildren out on trolley and shore trips. With the Christian Endeavor, the Epworth League, and kindred societies looking about for something to try their young strength and enthusiasm on, we may be here standing upon the threshold of something which shall bring us nearer to a universal brotherhood than all the consecrations and badges that have yet been invented.

The mere contact with nature, even out of a barrel, brought something to those starved child lives that struck a new note. Sometimes it rang with a sharp and jarring sound. The boys in the Hester Street school could not be made to take an interest in the lesson on wheat until the teacher came to the effect of drought and a bad year on the farmer's pocket. Then they understood. They knew the process. Strikes cut into the earnings of Hester Street, small enough at the best of times, at frequent intervals, and the boys need not be told what a bad year means. No other kind ever occurs there. They learned the lesson on wheat in no time, after that. Oftener it was a gentler note that piped timidly in the strange place. A barrel of wild roses came one day, instead of the expected "specimens," and these were given to the children. They took them greedily. "I wondered," said the teacher, "if it was more love of the flower, or of getting something for nothing, no matter what." But even if it were largely the latter, there was still the rose. Nothing like it had come that way before, and without a doubt it taught its own lesson. The Italian child might have jumped for it more eagerly, but its beauty was not wasted in Jew-town, either. The baby kissed it, and it lay upon more than one wan cheek, and whispered who knows what thought of hope and courage that were nearly gone. Even in Hester Street the wild rose from the hedge was not wasted.

The result of it all was wholesome and good, because it was common sense. The way to fight the slum in the children's lives is with sunlight and flowers and play, which their child hearts crave, if their eyes have never seen them. The teachers reported that the boys were easier to manage, more quiet, and played more fairly than before. The police reports showed that fewer were arrested or run over in the streets than in other years. A worse enemy was attacked than the trolley car or the truck. In the kindergarten at the Hull House in Chicago there hangs a picture of a harvest scene, with the man wiping his brow, and a woman resting at his feet. The teacher told me that a little girl with an old face picked it out among all the rest, and considered it long and gravely. "Well," she said, when her inspection was finished, "he knocked her down, didn't he?" A two hours' argument for kindergartens or vacation schools could not have put it stronger or better.

The awakening of the civic conscience is nowhere more plainly traced than in our public schools. The last five years have set us fifty years ahead, and there is now no doubling on the track we have struck. We have fifty kindergartens to-day where five years ago we had one, and their method has invaded the whole system of teaching. Cooking, the only kind of temperance preaching that counts for anything in a school course, is taught in the girls' classes. Five years ago a minister of justice declared in the Belgian Chamber that the nation was reverting to a new form of barbarism, which he described by the term "alcoholic barbarism," and pointed out as its first cause the "insufficiency of the food procurable by the working classes." He referred to the quality, not the quantity. The United States experts, who lately made a study of the living habits of the poor in New York, spoke of it as a common observation that "a not inconsiderable amount of the prevalent intemperance can be traced to poor food and unattractive home tables." The toasting-fork in Jacob's sister's hand beats preaching in the campaign against the saloon, just as the boys' club beats the police club in fighting the gang.

The cram and the jam are being crowded out as common-sense teaching steps in and takes their place, and the "three H's," the head, the heart, and the hand,--a whole boy,--are taking the place too long monopolized by the "three R's." There was need of it. It had seemed sometimes as if, in our anxiety lest he should not get enough, we were in danger of stuffing the boy to the point of making a hopeless dunce of him. It is a higher function of the school to teach principles than to impart facts merely. Teaching the boy municipal politics and a thousand things to make a good citizen of him, instead of so filling him with love of his country and pride in its traditions that he is bound to take the right stand when the time comes, is as though one were to attempt to put all the law of the state into its constitution to make it more binding. The result would be hopeless congestion and general uselessness.

It comes down to the teacher in the end, and there are 5600 of them in the old city alone, 10,000 for the greater city;[7] the great mass faithful and zealous, but yoked to the traditions of a day that is past. Half the machine teaching, the wooden output of our public schools in the past, I believe was due to the practical isolation of the teachers between the tyranny of politics and the distrust of those who had good cause to fear the politician and his work. There was never a more saddening sight than that of the teachers standing together in an almost solid body to resist reform of the school system as an attack upon them. There was no pretense on their part that the schools did not need reform. They knew better. They fought for their places. Throughout the fight no word came from them of the children's rights. They imagined that theirs were in danger, and they had no thought for anything else. We gathered then the ripe fruit of politics, and it will be a long while, I suppose, before we get the taste out of our mouths. But the grip of politics on our schools has been loosened, if not shaken off altogether, and the teacher's slavery is at an end, if she herself so wills it. Once hardly thought worthy of a day laborer's hire, she will receive a policeman's pay for faithful service[8] in the school year now begun, with his privilege of a half-pay pension on retirement. Within three weeks after the passage of the salary bill forty-two teachers in the boroughs of Manhattan and Bronx had applied for retirement. The training schools are hard at work filling up the gaps. The windows of the schoolhouse have been thrown open, and life let in there too with the sunlight. The day may be not far distant when ours shall be schools "for discovering aptitude," in Professor Felix Adler's wise plan. The problem is a vast one, even in its bulk; every year seats must be found on the school benches for twenty thousand additional children. However deep we have gone down into our pockets to pay for new schools, there are to-day in the greater city nearly thirty thousand children in half-day or part-time classes, waiting their chance. But that it can and will be solved the experience of the last five years fully warrants.

[Footnote 7: The exact number for April, 1899, was 9989; number of pupils registered, 401,761; average daily attendance, 370,722.]

[Footnote 8: The teacher's pay, under the new act, is from $600 to $1400. The policeman's pay is $1400.]

In the solution the women of New York will have had no mean share. In the struggle for school reform they struck the telling blows, and the credit for the victory was justly theirs. The Public Education Association, originally a woman's auxiliary to Good Government Club E, has since worked as energetically with the school authorities as it before worked against them. It has opened many windows for little souls by hanging schoolrooms with beautiful casts and pictures, and forged at the same time new and strong links in the chain that bound the boy all too feebly to the school. At a time when the demand of the boys of the East Side for club room, which was in itself one of the healthiest signs of the day, had reached an exceedingly dangerous pass, the Public Education Association broke ground that will prove the most fertile field of all. The Raines law saloon, quick to discern in the new demand the gap that would divorce it by and by from the man, attempted to bridge it by inviting the boy in under its roof. Occasionally the girl went along. A typical instance of how the scheme worked was brought to my attention at the time by the manager of the College Settlement. The back room of the saloon was given to the club free of charge, with the understanding that the boy members should "treat." As a means of raising the needed funds, the club hit upon the plan of fining members ten cents when they "got funny." To defeat this device of the devil some way must be found; but club room was scarce among the tenements. The Good Government Clubs proposed to the Board of Education that it open the empty class-rooms at night for the children's use. It was my privilege to plead their cause before the School Board, and to obtain from it the necessary permission, after some hesitation and doubt as to whether "it was educational." The Public Education Association promptly assumed the responsibility for "the property," and the Hester Street school was opened. There are now two schools that are given over to evening clubs. The property has not been molested, but the boys who have met under Miss Winifred Buck's management have learned many a lesson of self-control and practical wisdom that has proved "educational" in the highest degree. Her plan is simplicity itself. Through their play--the meeting usually begins with a romp-- in quarters where there is not too much elbow-room, the boys learn the first lesson of respecting one another's rights. The subsequent business meeting puts them upon the fundamentals of civilized society, as it were. Out of the debate of the question, Do we want boys who swear, steal, gamble, and smoke cigarettes? grow convictions as to why these vices are wrong that put "the gang" in its proper light. Punishment comes to appear, when administered by the boys themselves, a natural consequence of law-breaking, in defense of society; and the boy is won. He can thenceforward be trusted to work out his own salvation. If he does it occasionally with excessive unction, remember how recent is his conversion. "Resolved, that wisdom is better than wealth," was rejected as a topic for discussion by one of the clubs, because "everybody knows it is." This was in the Tenth Ward. If temptation had come that way in the shape of a pushcart with pineapples--we are all human! Anyway, they had learned the right.

With the women to lead, the school has even turned the tables on the jail and invaded it bodily. For now nearly two years the Public Education Association has kept school in the Tombs, for the boys locked up there awaiting trial. Of thirty-one pupils on this school register, the other day, twelve were charged with burglary, four with highway robbery, and three with murder. That was the gang run to earth at last. Better late than never.

The windows of their prison overlooked the spot where the gallows used to stand that cut short many a career such as they pursued. They were soberly attentive to their studies, which were of a severely practical turn. Their teacher, Mr. David Willard, who was a resident of the University Settlement in its old Delancey Street home,--the fact that the forces for good one finds at work in the slum usually lead back to the settlements shows best that they have so far escaped the peril of stiffening into mere institutions,--has his own sound view of how to head off the hangman. Daily and nightly he gathers about him in the house on Chrystie Street, where he makes his home, three hundred boys and girls, whom he meets as their friend, on equal terms. The club is the means of getting them there, and so it is in its right place.

Once a week another teacher comes to the Tombs school, and tells the boys of our city's history, its famous buildings and great men; trying so to arouse their interest as a first step toward a citizen's pride. This one also is sent by a club of women, the City History Club, which in three years has done strange things among the children. It sprang from the proposition of Mr. Robert Abbe that the man and the citizen has his birth in the boy, and that to love a thing one must know it first. The half-dozen classes that were started for the study of our city's history have swelled into nearly a hundred, with quite eighteen hundred pupils. The pregnant fact was noted early by the teachers, that the immigrant boy easily outstrips in interest for his adopted home the native, who perchance turns up his nose at him, and later very likely complains of the "unscrupulousness" of the Jew who forged ahead of him in business as well.

"Everything takes ten years." Looking back from the closing year of the century, one is almost tempted to turn Mr. Hewitt's phrase about, and say that everything has been packed into ten years. The tenth winter of the free lectures, which the city provides to fill up in a measure those gaps which the earlier years left, has just passed. When the first course showed an attendance of 22,149 upon 186 lectures, we were all encouraged; but the last season saw 1923 lectures delivered upon every topic of human interest, from the care of our bodies and natural science to literature, astronomy, and music, and a multitude of 519,411 persons, chiefly workingmen and their wives, the parents of the schoolboy, heard them. Forty-eight schools and halls were employed for the purpose. The People's Institute adds to this programme a forum for the discussion of social topics, nineteenth-century history, and "present problems" on a wholly non-partisan, unsectarian basis. The Institute was launched upon its educational mission within six weeks after the disastrous Greater New York election in 1897. It has since drawn to the platform of the Cooper Institute audiences, chiefly of workingmen more or less connected with the labor movement, that have filled its great hall. The spirit that animates its work is shown in its review of the field upon the threshold of its third year. Speaking of the social issues that are hastening toward a settlement, it says: "Society is about to be organized, gradually, wisely, on the lines of the recognition of the brotherhood of man. The People's Institute holds to-day, as no other institution in this city, the confidence of all classes of the working people; also of the best minds among the well-to-do classes. It can throw all its influence upon the side of removing misunderstandings, promoting mutual confidence.... This is its great work." A great undertaking, truly, but one in which no one may rashly say it shall not succeed. As an installment, it organized last spring, for study, discussion, and social intercourse, the first of a chain of People's Clubs, full of a strong and stirring life, which within three months had a membership of three hundred and fifty, and a list of two hundred and fifty applicants.

While the Institute's plan has met with this cordial reception downtown, uptown, among the leisure classes, its acceptance has been nothing like so ready. Selfish wealth has turned a cold shoulder to the brotherhood of man, as so often in the past. Still the proffered hand is not withdrawn. In a hundred ways it is held out with tender of help and sympathy and friendship, these days, where distrust and indifference were once the rule. The People's University Extension Society, leaving the platform to its allies, invades the home, the nursery, the kindergarten, the club, wherever it can, with help and counsel. Down on the lower East Side, the Educational Alliance conducts from the Hebrew Institute an energetic campaign among the Jewish immigrants that reaches fully six thousand souls, two thirds of them children, every day in the week. Sixty-two clubs alone hold meetings in the building on Saturday and Sunday. Under the same roof the Baron Hirsch Fund has taught sixteen thousand children of refugee Jews in nine years. It passes them on to the public schools within six months of their landing, the best material they receive from anywhere.

So the boy is being got ready for dealing, in the years that are to come, with the other but not more difficult problems of setting his house to rights, and ridding it of the political gang which now misrepresents him and us. And justice to Jacob is being evolved. Not yet without obstruction and dragging of feet. The excellent home library plan that proved so wholesome in the poor quarters of Boston has failed in New York, except in a few notable instances, through the difficulty of securing the visitors upon whom the plan depends for its success. The same want has kept the boys' club from reaching the development that would apply the real test to it as a barrier against the slum. There are fifteen clubs for every Winifred Buck that is in sight. From the City History Club, the Charity Organization Society, from everywhere, comes the same complaint. The hardest thing in the world to give is still one's self. But it is all the time getting to be easier. There are daily more women and men who, thinking of the boy, can say, and do, with my friend of the College Settlement, when an opportunity to enter a larger field was offered her, "No, I am content to stay here, to be ready for Johnnie when he wants me."

Justice for the boy, and for his father. An itinerant Jewish glazier, crying his wares, was beckoned into a stable by the foreman, and bidden to replace a lot of broken panes, enough nearly to exhaust his stock. When, after working half the day, he asked for his pay, he was driven from the place with jeers and vile words. Raging and impotent, he went back to his poor tenement cursing a world in which there was no justice for a poor man. If he had next been found ranting with anarchists against the social order, would you have blamed him? He found instead, in the Legal Aid Society, a champion that pleaded his cause and compelled the stableman to pay him his wages. For a hundred thousand such--more shame to us--this society has meant all that freedom promised: justice to the poor man. It too has earned a place among the forces that are working out through the new education the brighter day, for it has taught the lesson which all the citizens of a free state need most to learn,--respect for law.

VIII

REFORM BY HUMANE TOUCH

I have sketched in outline the gains achieved in the metropolis since its conscience awoke. Now, in closing this account, I am reminded of the story of an old Irishman who died here a couple of years ago. Patrick Mullen was an honest blacksmith. He made guns for a living. He made them so well that one with his name on it was worth a good deal more than the market price of guns. Other makers went to him with offers of money for the use of his stamp; but they never went twice. When sometimes a gun of very superior make was brought to him to finish, he would stamp it P. Mullen, never Patrick Mullen. Only to that which he himself had wrought did he give his honest name without reserve. When he died, judges and bishops and other great men crowded to his modest home by the East River, and wrote letters to the newspapers telling how proud they had been to call him friend. Yet he was, and remained to the end, plain Patrick Mullen, blacksmith and gunmaker.

In his life he supplied the answer to the sigh of dreamers in all days: when will the millennium come? It will come when every man is a Patrick Mullen at his own trade; not merely a P. Mullen, but a Patrick Mullen. The millennium of municipal politics, when there shall be no slum to fight, will come when every citizen does his whole duty as a citizen; not before. As long as he "despises politics," and deputizes another to do it for him, whether that other wears the stamp of a Croker or of a Platt,--it matters little which,--we shall have the slum, and be put periodically to the trouble and the shame of draining it in the public sight. A citizen's duty is one thing that cannot be farmed out safely; and the slum is not limited by the rookeries of Mulberry or Ludlow streets. It has long roots that feed on the selfishness and dullness of Fifth Avenue quite as greedily as on the squalor of the Sixth Ward. The two are not nearly so far apart as they look.

I am not saying this because it is anything new, but because we have just had an illustration of its truth in municipal politics. Waring and Roosevelt were the Patrick Mullens of the reform administration which Tammany has now replaced with her insolent platform, "To hell with reform." It was not an ideal administration, but it can be said of it, at least, that it was up to the times it served. It made compromises with spoils politics, and they were wretched failures. It took Waring and Roosevelt on the other plan, on which they insisted, of divorcing politics from the public business, and they let in more light than even my small parks over on the East Side. For they showed us where we stood and what was the matter with us. We believed in Waring when he demonstrated the success of his plan for cleaning the streets: not before. When Roosevelt announced his programme of enforcing the excise law because it was law, a howl arose that would have frightened a less resolute man from his purpose. But he went right on doing the duty he was sworn to do. And when, at the end of three months of clamor and abuse, we saw the spectacle of the saloon keepers formally resolving to help the police instead of hindering them; of the prison ward in Bellevue Hospital standing empty for three days at a time, an astonishing and unprecedented thing, which the warden could only attribute to the "prompt closing of the saloons at one A. M.;" and of the police force recovering its lost self-respect, we had found out more and greater things than whether the excise law was a good or a bad law. We understood what Roosevelt meant when he insisted upon the "primary virtues" of honesty and courage in the conduct of public business. For the want of them in us, half the laws that touched our daily lives had become dead letters or vehicles of blackmail and oppression. It was worth something to have that lesson taught us in that way; to find out that simple, straightforward, honest dealing as between man and man is after all effective in politics as in gunmaking. Perhaps we have not mastered the lesson yet. But we have not discharged the teacher, either.

Courage, indeed! There were times during that stormy spell when it seemed as if we had grown wholly and hopelessly flabby as a people. All the outcry against the programme of order did not come from the lawless and the disorderly, by any means. Ordinarily decent, conservative citizens joined in counseling moderation and virtual compromise with the law-breakers--it was nothing else--to "avoid trouble." The old love of fair play had been whittled down by the jackknife of all-pervading expediency to an anaric desire to "hold the scales even;" that is a favorite modern device of the devil for paralyzing action in men. You cannot hold the scales even in a moral issue. It inevitably results in the triumph of evil, which asks nothing better than the even chance to which it is not entitled. When the trouble in the Police Board had reached a point where it seemed impossible not to understand that Roosevelt and his side were fighting a cold and treacherous conspiracy against the cause of good government, we had the spectacle of a Christian Endeavor Society inviting the man who had hatched the plot, the bitter and relentless enemy whom the Mayor had summoned to resign, and afterward did his best to remove as a fatal obstacle to reform,--inviting this man to come before it and speak of Christian citizenship! It was a sight to make the bosses hug themselves with glee. For Christian citizenship is their nightmare, and nothing is so cheering to them as evidence that those who profess it have no sense.

Apart from the moral bearings of it, what this question of enforcement of law means in the life of the poor was illustrated by testimony given before the Police Board very recently. A captain was on trial for allowing the policy swindle to go unchecked in his precinct. Policy is a kind of penny lottery, with alleged daily drawings which never take place. The whole thing is a pestilent fraud, which is allowed to exist only because it pays heavy blackmail to the police and the politicians. Expert witnesses testified that eight policy shops in the Twenty-First Ward, which they had visited, did a business averaging about thirty-two dollars a day each. The Twenty-First is a poor Irish tenement ward. The policy sharks were getting two hundred and fifty dollars or more a day of the hard-earned wages of those poor people, in sums of from one and two cents to a quarter, without making any return for it. The thing would seem incredible, were it not too sadly familiar. The saloon keeper got his share of what was left, and rewarded his customer by posing as the "friend of the poor man" whenever his business was under scrutiny; I have yet in my office the record of a single week during the hottest of the fight between Roosevelt and the saloons, as showing of what kind that friendship is. It embraces the destruction of eight homes by the demon of drunkenness: the suicide of four wives, the murder of two others by drunken husbands, the killing of a policeman in the street, and the torture of an aged woman by her rascal son, who "used to be a good boy till he took to liquor, when he became a perfect devil." In that role he finally beat her to death for giving shelter to some evicted fellow tenants who else would have had to sleep in the street. Nice friendly turn, wasn't it?

And yet there was something to be said for the saloon keeper. He gave the man the refuge from his tenement which he needed. I say needed, purposely. There has been a good deal of talk lately about the saloon as a social necessity. About all there is to that is that the saloon is there, and the necessity too. Man is a social animal, whether he lives in a tenement or in a palace. But the palace has resources; the tenement has not. It is a good place to get away from at all times. The saloon is cheery and bright, and never far away. The man craving human companionship finds it there. He finds, too, in the saloon keeper one who understands his wants much better than the reformer who talks civil service in the meetings. "Civil service" to him and his kind means yet a contrivance for keeping them out of a job. The saloon keeper knows the boss, if he is not himself the boss or his lieutenant, and can steer him to the man who will spend all day at the City Hall, if need be, to get a job for a friend, and all night pulling wires to keep him in it, if trouble is brewing. Mr. Beecher used to say, when pleading for bright hymn tunes, that he didn't want the devil to have the monopoly of all the good music in the world. The saloon has had the monopoly up to date of all the cheer in the tenements. If its owner has made it pan out to his own advantage and the boss's, we at least have no just cause of complaint. We let him have the field all to himself.

As to this boss, of whom we hear so much, what manner of man is he? That depends on how you look at him. I have one in mind, a district boss, whom you would accept instantly as a type, if I were to mention his name, which I shall not do for a reason which I fear will shock you: he and I are friends. In his private capacity I have real regard for him. As a politician and a boss I have none at all. I am aware that this is taking low ground in a discussion of this kind, but perhaps the reader will better understand the relations of his "district" to him, if I let him into mine. There is no political bond between us, of either district or party; just the reverse. It is purely personal. He was once a police justice,--at that time he kept a saloon,--and I never knew one with more common sense, which happens to be the one quality especially needed in that office. Up to the point where politics came in I could depend upon him entirely. At that point he let me know bluntly that he was in the habit of running his district to suit himself. The way he did it brought him under the just accusation of being guilty of every kind of rascality known to politics. When next our paths would cross each other, it would very likely be on some errand of mercy, to which his feet were always swift. I recall the distress of a dear and gentle lady at whose dinner table I once took his part. She could not believe that there was any good in him; what he did must be done for effect. Some time after that she wrote asking me to look after an East Side family that was in great trouble. It was during the severe cold spell of last winter, and there was need of haste. I went over at once; but although I had lost no time, I found my friend the boss ahead of me. It was a real pleasure to me to be able to report to my correspondent that he had seen to their comfort, and to add that it was unpolitical charity altogether. The family was that of a Jewish widow with a lot of little children. He is a Roman Catholic. There were no men, consequently no voters, in the house, which was far outside of his district, too; and as for effect, he was rather shamefaced at my catching him at it. I do not believe that a soul has ever heard of the case from him to this day.

My friend is a Tammany boss. During that same cold spell a politician of the other camp came into my office and gave me a hundred dollars to spend as I saw fit among the poor. His district was miles uptown, and he was most unwilling to disclose his identity, stipulating in the end that no one but I should know where the money came from. He was not seeking notoriety. The plight of the suffering had appealed to him, and he wanted to help where he could, that was all.

Now, I have not the least desire to glorify the boss in this. He is not glorious to me. He is simply human. Often enough he is a coarse and brutal fellow, in his morals as in his politics. Again, he may have some very engaging personal traits that bind his friends to him with the closest of ties. The poor man sees the friend, the charity, the power that is able and ready to help him in need; is it any wonder that he overlooks the source of this power, this plenty,--that he forgets the robbery in the robber who is "good to the poor"? Anyhow, if anybody got robbed, it was "the rich." With the present ethical standards of the slum, it is easy to construct even a scheme of social justice out of it that is very comforting all round, even to the boss himself, though he is in need of no sympathy or excuse. "Politics," he will tell me in his philosophic moods, "is a game for profit. The city foots the bills." Patriotism means to him working for the ticket that shall bring more profit. "I regard," he says, lighting his cigar, "a repeater as a shade off a murderer, but you are obliged to admit that in my trade he is a necessary evil." I am not obliged to do anything of the kind, but I can understand his way of looking at it. He simply has no political conscience. He has gratitude, loyalty to a friend,--that is part of his stock in trade,--fighting blood, plenty of it, all the good qualities of the savage; nothing more. And a savage he is, politically, with no soul above the dross. He would not rob a neighbor for the world; but he will steal from the city-- though he does not call it by that name--without a tremor, and count it a good mark. When I tell him that, he waves his hand toward Wall Street as representative of the business community, and toward the office of his neighbor, the padrone, as representative of the railroads, and says with a laugh, "Don't they all do it?"

The boss believes in himself. It is one of his strong points. And he has experience to back him. In the fall of 1894 we shook off boss rule in New York, and set up housekeeping for ourselves. We kept it up three years, and then went back to the old style. I should judge that we did it because we were tired of too much virtue. Perhaps we were not built to hold such a lot at once.

Besides, it is much easier to be ruled than to rule. That fall, after the election, when I was concerned about what would become of my small parks, of the Health Department in which we took such just pride, and of a dozen other things, I received one unvarying reply to my anxious question, or rather two. If it was the Health Department, I was told: "Go to Platt. He is the only man who can do it. He is a sensible man, and will see that it is protected." If small parks, it was: "Go to Croker. He will not allow the work to be stopped." A playgrounds bill was to be presented in the legislature, and everybody advised: "Go to Platt. He won't have any objection: it is popular." And so on. My advisers were not politicians. They were business men, but recently honestly interested in reform. I was talking one day with a gentleman of very wide reputation as a philanthropist, about the unhappy lot of the old fire-engine horses,--which, after lives of toil that deserve a better fate, are sold for a song to drag out a weary existence hauling some huckster's cart around,--and wishing that they might be pensioned off to live out their years on a farm, with enough to eat and a chance to roll in the grass. He was much interested, and promptly gave me this advice: "I tell you what you do. You go and see Croker. He likes horses." No wonder the boss believes in himself. He would be less than human if he did not. And he is very human.

I had voted on the day of the Greater New York election,--the Tammany election, as we learned to call it afterward,--in my home out in the Borough of Queens, and went over to the depot to catch the train for the city. On the platform were half a dozen of my neighbors, all business men, all "friends of reform." Some of them were just down from breakfast. One I remembered as introducing a resolution, in a meeting we had held, about the discourtesy of local politicians. He looked surprised when reminded that it was election day. "Why, is it to-day?" he said. "They didn't send any carriage," said another regretfully. "I don't see what's the use," said the third; "the roads are just as bad as when we began talking about it." (We had been trying to mend them.) The fourth yawned and said: "I don't care. I have my business to attend to." And they took the train, which meant that they lost their votes. The Tammany captain was busy hauling his voters by the cartload to the polling place. Over there stood a reform candidate who had been defeated in the primary, and puffed out his chest. "The politicians are afraid of me," he said. They slapped him on the back, as they went by, and told him that he was a devil of a fellow.

So Tammany came back. The Health Department is wrecked. The police force is worse than before Roosevelt took hold of it, and we are back in the mud out of which we pulled ourselves with such an effort. And we are swearing at it. But I am afraid we are swearing at the wrong fellow. The real Tammany is not the conscienceless rascal that plunders our treasury and fattens on our substance. That one is a mere counterfeit. It is the voter who waits for a carriage to take him to the polls, the man who "doesn't see what's the use;" the business man who says "business is business," and has no time to waste on voting; the citizen who "will wait to see how the cat jumps, because he doesn't want to throw his vote away;" the cowardly American who "doesn't want to antagonize" anybody; the fool who "washes his hands of politics." These are the real Tammany, the men after the boss's own heart. For every one whose vote he buys, there are two of these who give him theirs for nothing. We shall get rid of him when these withdraw their support, when they become citizens of the Patrick Mullen stamp, as faithful at the polling place as he was at the forge; not before.

The true work of reform is at the top, not at the bottom. The man in the slum votes according to his light, and the boss holds the candle. But the boss is in no real sense a leader. He follows instead, always as far behind the moral sentiment of the community as he thinks is safe. He has heard it said that a community will not be any better than its citizens, and that it will be just as good as they are, and he applies the saying to himself. He is no worse a boss than the town deserves. I can conceive of his taking credit to himself as some kind of a moral instrument by which the virtue of the community may be graded, though that is most unlikely. He does not bother himself with the morals of anything. But right here is his Achilles heel. The man has no conscience. He cannot tell the signs of it in others. It always comes upon him unawares. Reform to him simply means the "outs" fighting to get in. The real thing he will always underestimate. Such a man is not the power he seems. He is formidable only in proportion to the amount of shaking it takes to rouse the community's conscience.

The boss is like the measles, a distemper of a self-governing people's infancy. When we shall have come of age politically, he will have no terrors for us. Meanwhile, being charged with the business of governing, which we left to him because we were too busy making money, he follows the track laid out for him, and makes the business pan out all that is in it. He fights when we want to discharge him. Of course he does. No man likes to give up a good job. He will fight or bargain, as he sees his way clear. He will give us small parks, play piers, new schools, anything we ask, to keep his place, while trying to find out "the price" of this conscience which he does not understand. Even to the half of his kingdom he will give, to be "in" on the new deal. He has done it before, and there is no reason that he can see why it should not be done again. And he will appeal to the people whom he is plundering to trust him because they know him.

Odd as it sounds, this is where he has his real hold. I have shown why this is so. To the poor people of his district the boss is a real friend in need. He is one of them. He does not want to reform them; far from it. No doubt it is very ungrateful of them, but the poor people have no desire to be reformed. They do not think they need to be. They consider their moral standards quite as high as those of the rich, and resent being told that they are mistaken. The reformer comes to them from another world to tell them these things, and goes his way. The boss lives among them. He helped John to a job on the pipes in their hard winter, and got Mike on the force. They know him as a good neighbor, and trust him to their harm. He drags their standard ever farther down. The question for those who are trying to help them is how to make them transfer their allegiance, and trust their real friends instead.

It ought not to be a difficult question to answer. Any teacher could do it. He knows, if he knows anything, that the way to get and keep the children's confidence is to trust them, and let them know that they are trusted. They will almost always come up to the demand thus made upon them. Preaching to them does little good; preaching at them still less. Men, whether rich or poor, are much like children. The good in them is just as good as it is said to be, and the bad, considering their enlarged opportunities for mischief, not so much worse than it is called. A vigorous optimism, a stout belief in one's fellow man, is better equipment in a campaign for civic virtue than stacks of tracts and arguments, economic and moral, are. There is good bottom, even in the slum, for that kind of an anchor to get a grip on. A year ago I went to see a boxing match there had been much talk about. The hall was jammed with a rough and noisy crowd, hotly intent upon its favorite. His opponent, who hailed, I think, from somewhere in Delaware, was greeted with hostile demonstrations as a "foreigner." But as the battle wore on, and he was seen to be fair and manly, while the New Yorker struck one foul blow after another, the attitude of the crowd changed rapidly from enthusiastic approval of the favorite to scorn and contempt; and in the last round, when he knocked the Delawarean over with a foul blow, the audience rose in a body and yelled to have the fight given to the "foreigner," until my blood tingled with pride. For the decision would leave it practically without a cent. It had staked all it had on the New Yorker. "He is a good man," I heard on all sides, while the once favorite sneaked away without a friend. "Good" meant fair and manly to that crowd. I thought, as I went to the office the next morning, that it ought to be easy to appeal to such a people with measures that were fair and just, if we could only get on common ground. But the only hint I got from my reform paper was an editorial denunciation of the brutality of boxing, on the same page that had an enthusiastic review of the college football season. I do not suppose it did any harm, for the paper was probably not read by one of the men it had set out to reform. But suppose it had been, how much would it have appealed to them? Exactly the qualities of robust manliness which football is supposed to encourage in college students had been evoked by the trial of strength and skill which they had witnessed. As to the brutality, they knew that fifty young men are maimed or killed at football to one who fairs ill in a boxing match. Would it seem to them common sense, or cant and humbug?

It comes down in the end to a question of common sense and common honesty. For how many failures of reform effort is insincerity not to blame! Last spring I attended a meeting at Albany that had been called by the governor to discuss the better enforcement of the labor laws. We talked the situation over, and Mr. Roosevelt received from those present their ready promise to aid him in every way in making effective the laws that represented so much toil and sacrifice, yet had until then been in too many instances barren of results. Some time after, a workingman told me with scorn how, on our coming home, one of our party had stopped in at the factory inspector's office to urge him to "let up" on a friend, a cigar manufacturer, who was violating a law for which the labor organizations had fought long years as absolutely necessary to secure human conditions in the trade. How much stock might he and his fellows be supposed to take in a movement that had such champions? "You scratch my back and I'll scratch yours," is a kind of politics in which the reformer is no match for the boss. The boss will win on that line every time. A saving sense of humor might have avoided that and many other pitfalls. I am seriously of the opinion that a professional humorist ought to be attached to every reform movement, to keep it from making itself ridiculous by either too great solemnity or too much conceit. As it is, the enemy sometimes employs him with effect. Failing the adoption of that plan, I would recommend a decree of banishment against photographers, press-clippings men, and the rest of the congratulatory staff. Why should the fact that a citizen has done a citizen's duty deserve to be celebrated in print and picture, as if something extraordinary had happened? The smoke of battle had not cleared away after the victory of reform, in the fall of 1894, before the citizens' committee and all the little sub-committees rushed pell-mell to the photographer's to get themselves on record as the men who did it. The spectacle might have inspired in the humorist the advice to get two sets made, while they were about it,--one to serve by and by as an exhibit of the men who didn't; and, as the event proved, he would have been right.

But it is easy to find fault, and on that tack we get no farther. Those men did a great work, and they did it well. The mile-posts they set up on the road to better things will guide another generation to the goal, however the present may go astray. Good schools, better homes, and a chance for the boy are arguments that are not lost upon the people. They wear well. It may be that, like Moses and his followers, we of the present day shall see the promised land only from afar and with the eye of faith, because of our sins; that to a younger and sturdier to-morrow it shall be given to blaze the path of civic righteousness that was our dream. I like to think that it is so, and that that is the meaning of the coming of men like Roosevelt and Waring at this time with their simple appeal to the reason of honest men. Unless I greatly err in reading the signs of the times, it is indeed so, and the day of the boss and of the slum is drawing to an end. Our faith has felt the new impulse; rather, I should say, it has given it. The social movements, and that which we call politics, are but a reflection of what the people honestly believe, a chart of their aims and aspirations. Charity in our day no longer means alms, but justice. The social settlements are substituting vital touch for the machine charity that reaped a crop of hate and beggary. They are passenger bridges, it has been truly said, not mere "shoots" for the delivery of coal and groceries; bridges upon which men go over, not down, from the mansion to the tenement. We have learned that we cannot pass off checks for human sympathy in settlement of our brotherhood arrears. The church, which once stood by indifferent, or worse, is hastening to enter the life of the people. In the memory of men yet living, one church, moving uptown away from the crowd, left its old Mulberry Street home to be converted into tenements that justly earned the name of "dens of death" in the Health Department's records, while another became the foulest lodging house in an unclean city. It was a church corporation which in those bad days owned the worst underground dive downtown, and turned a deaf ear to all remonstrances. The church was "angling for souls." But souls in this world live in bodies endowed with reason. The results of that kind of fishing were empty pews and cold hearts, and the conscience-stricken cry that went up, "What shall we do to lay hold of this great multitude that has slipped from us?"

Ten years have passed, and to-day we see the churches of every denomination uniting in a systematic canvass of the city to get at the facts of the people's life of which they had ceased to be a part, pleading for parks, playgrounds, kindergartens, libraries, clubs, and better homes. There is a new and hearty sound to the word "brother" that is full of hope. The cry has been answered. The gap in the social body, between rich and poor, is no longer widening. We are certainly coming closer together. Ten years ago, when the King's Daughters lighted a Christmas tree in Gotham Court, the children ran screaming from Santa Claus as from a "bogey man." Last Christmas the boys in the Hebrew Institute's schools nearly broke the bank laying in supplies to do him honor. I do not mean that the Jews are deserting to join the Christian church. They are doing that which is better,--they are embracing its spirit; and they and we are the better for it. God knows we waited long enough; and how close we were to each other all the while without knowing it! Last Christmas a clergyman, who lives out of town and has a houseful of children, asked me if I could not find for them a poor family in the city with children of about the same ages, whom they might visit and befriend. He worked every day in the office of a foreign mission in Fifth Avenue, and knew little of the life that moved about him in the city. I picked out a Hungarian widow in an East Side tenement, whose brave struggle to keep her little flock together had enlisted my sympathy and strong admiration. She was a cleaner in an office building; not until all the arrangements had been made did it occur to me to ask where. Then it turned out that she was scrubbing floors in the missionary society's house, right at my friend's door. They had passed each other every day, each in need of the other, and each as far from the other as if oceans separated them instead of a doorstep four inches wide.

* * * * *

Looking back over the years that lie behind with their work, and forward to those that are coming, I see only cause for hope. As I write these last lines in a far distant land, in the city of my birth, the children are playing under my window, and calling to one another with glad cries in my sweet mother tongue, even as we did in the long ago. Life and the world are before them, bright with the promise of morning. So to me seem the skies at home. Not lightly do I say it, for I have known the toil of rough-hewing it on the pioneer line that turns men's hair gray; but I have seen also the reward of the toil. New York is the youngest of the world's great cities, barely yet out of its knickerbockers. It may be that the dawning century will see it as the greatest of them all. The task that is set it, the problem it has to solve and which it may not shirk, is the problem of civilization, of human progress, of a people's fitness for self-government that is on trial among us. We shall solve it by the world-old formula of human sympathy, of humane touch. Somewhere in these pages I have told of the woman in Chicago who accounted herself the happiest woman alive because she had at last obtained a playground for her poor neighbors' children. "I have lived here for years," she said to me, "and struggled with principalities and powers, and have made up my mind that the most and the best I can do is to live right here with my people and smile with them,--keep smiling; weep when I must, but smile as long as I possibly can." And the tears shone in her gentle old eyes as she said it. When we have learned to smile and weep with the poor, we shall have mastered our problem. Then the slum will have lost its grip and the boss his job.

Until then, while they are in possession, our business is to hold taut and take in slack right along; never letting go for a moment.

www.ingramcontent.com/pod-product-compliance
Lightning Source LLC
Chambersburg PA
CBHW070357290526
45790CB00004B/1536